WHO IS LIVING YOUR DREAM?

TAKING CHARGE AND SEEKING CHANGE

WAQAS SHUAIB

In the name of God, the most merciful, the most kind.

I dedicate this book to my parents, without their love and prayers
I would be lost

To my wife - my strength and motivation

To my brother, for always being sensible and considerate

Table of Contents

Introduction

Do you ever wonder why various people can simultaneously have different interpretations and reactions to the same event? Why some people see opportunities or solutions while others simply see setbacks? Why a certain individual can make miracles out of adversity and others merely struggle through life? How is it that some seek refuge or guidance in spirituality, while others seek affirmation through deeds and learning? How one sees their dreams wash away, while others live it?

I am amazed by the way human beings develop. It is a topic I love to study, to watch and to embrace. It is part of who I am. I believe that life is designed to reward the deserving and not the merely desiring. Motivation is good, but it must be met by action and intent. Every person has these abilities within them, the ability to move from a present state to a better state, perhaps closer to our dreams. That's the good news. The better news is that there is no cut-off date at which to start. Now is a good time as any, and you can start living your dream rather than being a spectator and watching others do it for you. There is no such thing as personal perfection, but there is such a thing as personal excellence, and this is within reach for everyone.

We live in a great juncture in history, where the opportunity for achievement abounds. My goal with this book is to highlight the many ways in which you can carve a path for yourself, using the skills and attributes that reside within. The book pulls from personal experiences, advice from people at the pinnacle of their careers, books and similar sources of inspiration: I went from being an average lad to becoming a physician. By changing my personal approach, I was able to change my life, and it is only right that I pay forward my good fortune by sharing what I have learned; because if I can do it, I know you can too, and I want you to succeed, so that you can help others. And so it goes.

No matter who you are, no matter what age you are or what stage of life you are in, I believe I can reach out to you through my words. We all play at this game of life, but we each get only one turn at the table. Therefore I believe we all deserve to know how to play with the cards we are dealt.

The chapters of this book contain comprehensive stories and ideas incorporated into a select group of topics that will empower you to improve the overall emotional, mental and physical well-being. It will reshape parts of the character and attitude that you deem in need of redesigning, and by reaffirming those great qualities that you already possess.

These chapters illustrate the most critical qualities of success: financial, professional, emotional and social, so that you may emulate them yourself.

Its overarching purpose, in a word, is YOU. The best you—a healthier, well respected, well balanced, prosperous, successful and admired you. It is my hope that this book becomes the light that guides you to the place you heart has always desired. As you read through the material, please note that you, "the reader," are the motivation for the words laid out here. As I walk you through the experience of so many others, I hope to leave you with a wider spectrum of options to choose from. Now, prepare to elevate your game, and set your plans in action to start living your dream. Prepare to take charge and seek change.

Character

Ability therefore may take you to the top, but its character, which keeps you there. | John Wooden

Character emerges from the raw material that is you. We are not born with character, but it develops. It evolves as a result of the interactions between the pieces of existence that forms our mind, body and spirit, along with the circumstances and situations, which the world places in front of us. How we handle things depends on who we are and what we choose to do.

Character is not passive but rather is an active ingredient of success in all fields of life. It is character that guides behavior when all other defense mechanisms fail, and it is character that guides emotions - helping to make decisions in the face of uncertainty. The giants of history such as Alexander the Great relied on character to build confidence, to sharpen vision and to inspire dedication in those around him. But character is not the exclusive tool of generals and kings. All human beings have the capacity to form character from our raw material. No matter the age, wealth or place of origin, we all share common experiences and emotions, such as the disappointment or frustration we feel when faced with a setback, and the joy that comes with victory.

However, even with so much potential in common, what truly sets people apart is the way in which we go about resolving setbacks and overcoming roadblocks. We must strive to acquire the skills to tame and discipline any disappointments. Let us face our challenges and hurdles with a yearning to learn and grown from them. It is the only way to true happiness. In my years of studying people, I have found that many instead turn to materialism when faced with setbacks and falls in order to distract themselves from reality. Sadly the lesson is often missed. Character is not built during good times; character is built in the face of calamities. Hence, let us learn to become good students and take advantage of our downfalls to nurture our character. Let us not seek quick fixes as knee jerk reactions to calamities, let us ponder and grow. Let us understand.

Now there is of course nothing wrong with desire for a better life. However common wisdom warns to stand guard at the doorway of our mind where the quick-fix message seeks its entrance. There is more to be gained by investing time and resources into the building of character, rather than in chasing worldly goods in the belief that they are the solution. By building yourself into a truly great person, the worldly goods – the ones that you still truly need – will find you.

Children grow up imitating their parents and as they grow, imitation grows too. It is a necessary element of human nature; imitation makes people feel part of society, and teaches valuable skills along the way. Imitation is a way of communicating and integrating with others—it is seen in the way we greet each other or the way in which we react to news. It is through these forms of interactions and behavior adaptations that people develop character. There is a common expression that says a man is known by the company he keeps. This is incorrect, or at least incomplete. Most people represent the average of the five people they most frequently interact with. We therefore *become* the company we keep.

The dictionary defines character as the, "Mental and moral qualities distinctive to an individual." Character builds will, and will represents the power of doing. A strong character unconsciously makes virtue a necessity. Having character is like having pride, and pride is an appreciation for who you are. Character represents a set of disciplines which we follow every day, which in turn influence the hundreds of decisions we make each day. Character matures like fine wine, becoming deeper, more complex, yet more stable and valuable when kept in the right settings long enough. People who have well-formed character stand on the frontline, ready to be challenged. They emerge as leaders, demonstrating an unshakable confidence that inspires confidence in those who follow.

So the first question becomes, do you have the **courage** to face your fears and become the person you want to be?

Courage

Courage is rightly esteemed the first of human qualities, because it is the quality which guarantees all others | Winston Churchill

When I think of courage the first thing that comes to mind is all of the brave soldiers who serve our nation. I have never walked the battleground, and so I cannot share a first-hand story of gallant bravery. However, I have been blessed with knowing a man who overturned conventions of life against all odds; a man I take pride in calling my mentor.

This man had fractured his spine, which rendered him incapacitated for six months. He was disabled and immobilized inside a cervical halo from the neck down. He would lie in his bed day and night relying on others to feed him and care for him. Everyone he knew came to visit him and to express their sympathy. The doctors had declared only two possible outcomes: the first was paralysis for life and the other was death. When all of those around him who had first offered sympathy decided to give-up hope, he stayed determined. His personal belief was that he was going to walk again. He was going to bounce back and not just survive, but thrive. I am proud to tell you that today this man has a wonderful family and a prosperous career at Harvard University. He has received many awards of excellence in medicine and for his diligent work in communities and academic societies.

Most of us spend our entire lives worrying about health, financial status and work. We fear enduring financial hardship if someone we love becomes ill. We fear losing our jobs in an already competitive economy that offers no compassion and little opportunity. While our fears hover over us like dark clouds, we must remember that courage is action in the face of fear; and not the absence of fear. Fear may make us feel disheartened, but we are never without the option to act. No matter how hard our fears push us towards surrender, every one of us can dig deep and find a place to stand our ground. We can always, choose to act. Between the stimulus that causes fear and our response that leads us through the fearful situation, lies the choice we all have about how to respond. Fear is a natural emotion. Failure is a possible outcome.

It is possible for your dreams to become a reality. However, it takes courage to share these dreams with others and to invite them along on the journey. Iconic historical figures such as Mahatma Gandhi, Marcus Aurelius, Dr. Martin Luther King Jr., and Albert Einstein were all visionary and courageous people. They each had a personal dream, which was eventually embraced by millions of people. Gandhi challenged the authority of the entire British government using nothing but a peaceful walk across his own country. Marcus Aurelius taught how philosophy and reverence towards nature help further a cause more than armies and weapons. Dr. King taught the power of a dream when embraced and shared by millions, and Einstein, who may be remembered as a genius, actually taught more about perseverance and open-mindedness.

In 1955, during the Montgomery Bus Boycott, it was the courageous efforts of Rosa Parks that set in motion the freedom movement and earned her the title of the first lady of civil rights. She held her ground for a cause she believed in despite the fear she felt. She helped turn the tide of race discrimination in America, even though it meant standing up to a hostile government and violent men. She felt fear, but her character and courage pushed her through.

Learning to be courageous and standing up for what we believe is a powerful tool that sharpens character like a pencil destined to write out its own future. Many people fail in life because they do not believe in themselves. Instead they seek refuge in the courage of others. At worst, this is the path of a fool. At best, it represents a person underdeveloped and unwilling to live their potential.

We all have an inner voice that guides us through times of trial and tribulation. This is the voice that tells us that everything is going to be fine. It is called positive self-talk, and it is part of our instinct, our central autonomic nervous system. To set ourselves free we must embrace this voice, take it seriously, and believe in it. It is this voice that will help you move from the vague shapes of the unknown.

Think, for example, about a situation where you have to fire someone. Who is in the worse position? Certainly the person being fired must face the trauma of losing both job and dignity, but you would feel awful too, as you realize that you could be next. There is the fear of the unknown on both sides of the situation. It is within this fear-filled situation that life has given the opportunity to expand and improve. There is a liberation that comes from the event. The termination has happened. There is now no need to fear that it might happen. It has happened. This is when humans are at their best. It is now the time for the inner voice to ask proactively, to ask powerful questions such as, "where shall I start?" There are concrete steps to take towards a new future. Understanding and embracing reality is courage; it gives us all a chance to start over. For many this is a chance at redemption, and for others it symbolizes the power of self-recovery.

The greatest virtue in life is real courage that allows us to face facts and live beyond them. Never doubt your abilities out of fear of failing, but rather dismiss your fear, for it merely underestimates your true abilities.

Courage makes it easier to stay on the right side of the road, to be ethical; even in times of despair or doubt, or in other words, to be **honest**

3

Honesty

Honesty is the first chapter in the book of wisdom | Thomas Jefferson

When I was a child my mother would tell my brother and I the story about a dishonest milkman who worked in the small town where she grew up. For years, she said, she watched the milkman grow ever wealthier while many other people nearby struggled to put food on the table. She recalls hearing the milkman asking her father for a loan, supposedly to level out his debts. The loan was never paid back. The milkman grew rich and soon became a land-lord. He assigned the work of milk delivery to his employees. As days went by, the quality of the milk dwindled, yet its price rose higher – higher than anyone had ever paid before. A few months went by and to the surprise of my mother the dishonest milkman was back to selling milk himself. She asked her father about this matter to only find out that the milkman had lost his house and his savings to a fire caused by an electrical short circuit. She would see him weeping and would overhear him saying "God has punished me for being dishonest to my loyal customers."

The truth is, it is easy to make money by being dishonest. You may have heard many rags-to-riches stories, but what you don't know is how many moral values may have been sold thousands of times over in exchange for that wealth. The trouble with morals is that they lurk, even in the hearts of the most evil people. When morals are ignored or suppressed, they do not disappear. They bide their time, and re-emerge as guilt, in a size and intensity proportional to the original crime. Regret, resentment and guilt are poisons to the soul. People who cast aside honesty and morals to defeat the enemy of poverty or frustration basically drink their own poison.

People become more successful and stay happier when their tasks are fueled by honesty and integrity, and are done to the best of one's ability. Honesty and integrity go hand-in-hand. To do what was promised and to be there as promised both demonstrate integrity. Having unshakable moral principles defines a person as a trustworthy human being. Honesty in action corresponds with the honor of spoken words. A man who refuses to lie even in the gravest of situations is a man who grows stronger with age while others become frail, weak and bitter. A consistently honest person is something of a rarity, but the value of such a person far exceeds a large unethical herd.

Honesty and integrity come naturally to those who seek it. A person who is destined for greatness discovers these attributes inside him or herself and uses them well. Speaking the truth and acting true to yourself is always the first step. There are those who might refrain from telling the truth to those who they feel could not make any use of it. This does not mean they would lie to others, but simply, they would refrain from revealing the whole truth about something. However it is important to constantly remind yourself of the truth, regardless, because it always cultivates positive change.

Children can teach us many things, whether they mean to or not. I often take my nephew to the park and watch him play. Like most kids, he loves the monkey bars, and he also loves running through a gushing water fountain. One particular sunny day, I left my nephew to play as usual with other children, while I sat reading the editorial section of the *New York Times*. Suddenly I heard him scream. He had fallen while running. My heart was in my mouth and I was instantly afraid, with the worst-case scenarios flooding my mind. I found him lying on the ground with blood gushing from a cut on his forehead. As you can imagine, I panicked, and I picked him up and frantically ran for the hospital. As I reached the hospital, the emergency staff came to my aid and reassured me that everything was going to be fine. After a few minutes the nursing staff called me in as they needed my help to calm my frightened nephew. I held his hand and told him that he was going to make it and he immediately started to calm down. He simply needed to hear those reassuring words from someone whom he trusted. When I asked him if he believed me that he would be OK, he quietly nodded his head and closed his eyes as if to say, "I know you mean what you say, and I trust you." This moment made me realize that whenever we plant the seed of honesty, it is not long before we reap the reward of trust.

Honesty builds a center, which develops the strength to keep going when things get tough. When the going gets tough, that is when you must **persevere**...

4

Perseverance

I do not think that there is any other quality so essential to success of any kind as the quality of perseverance. It overcomes almost everything, even nature | John D. Rockefeller

My grandfather was always an early bird. His days would start earlier than anyone else and they would end later than anyone else. I always admired him for his hard work and I looked up to him for inspiration. I would often wake up around the same time as he would just so that I could accompany him on his morning walk. On many occasions, as we walked across the farms that belonged to his childhood friends, people would offer us luscious fruits and vegetables. My grandfather, however, would politely refuse the offer, and thank them for their genuine hospitality.

I could never understand why he would not let me have a mango, since it was completely acceptable to take something that was offered by a friend. Occasionally during our walks we would stop at my favorite mango tree and he would say, "If you can get up there, then you can have one of those mangos." For many months, this continued. We would walk, and we would stop at the mango tree. Sometimes he would repeat his words, sometimes not. But regardless of whether he actually spoke the words or not, I continued to hear them: "If you can get up there, then you can have one of those mangos." I did not climb. You see, at that time, my fear of failure was stronger than my desire for victory. Every time I would stare at that tree I knew deep inside how badly I wanted to climb. I wanted to satisfy my appetite for mangos, but also to satisfy my grandfather, and justify his pride in me.

One day the desire for victory won over my fear of failure and I finally decided to make my move and climb the tree. I fell, and I fell again. This was painful, but my grandfather was no quitter and he was not about to let me quit. However I, with the arrogance of a child, chose to emulate the fox in Aesop's fable of the *Fox and the Grapes*. I decided that the mangos were not yet ripe and that I did not need sour mangos. I decided to quit.

Grandfather had other plans though. He looked down at me and told me to roll up my sleeves, spit on my hands and find a firm grip on the tree. He told me to look for gnarls, knots or bark holes to start my climb. He said I should picture a monkey climbing a tree. While the image of a monkey climbing the tree was funny to me, what was not so funny was the imposing six-foot tall frame of my grandfather staring me down! I began to climb the tree and as I got up on that tree, I discovered a few very important lessons. First, climbing a tree is hard work. Second, spitting on your hands does nothing. Third, and the most important, while the fox of Aesop's fable might have been correct about avoiding unripe fruits, it failed to recognize that nature only makes things rich, ripe, and success-ful, after persistent work.

What I learned from my tree-climbing lesson was that success, like the mangos, may appear fully formed when we see it, but only those who have achieved it know that it arrives after much energy has been expended. Success does not come to those who simply wish for it. Life is designed to reward those who deserve it, and not those who just desire it. To achieve success we must learn to work for it; and both hard work and smart work are essential ingredi-ents. Success is a frame of mind, and to develop that frame of mind we must learn to rehearse, practice and stick to a plan. Often we fall short. Goals and dreams remain distant and unreachable; we feel there is no way out of our current misery. But what we must all understand is that we can only hit what we aim for. If we fail, we must try again. We must find better ways, clever ways, to knock at the door of success. Just keep knocking and then be prepared to walk through the door when it finally opens.

Perseverance is a quality that we can teach ourselves. But it is a trait that has many enemies. Not external enemies, but the enemies that live within. I am talking about bad habits. Fueled by fear and negativity, bad habits are like emotional demons that seek to dominate our actions. One of these is procrastination. It is amazing to observe people exert energy in planning recreational activities, yet avoid applying the same types of energies to reach their goals in life. Why is this? It is because leisure activities are seen as fun, and fun, by its very nature, is attractive. But serious tasks, or tasks with long-term payout, are often less pleasurable in the present. The human mind, dominated as it is by emotion, interprets less pleasurable tasks as fear-inducing since they carry a sense of unpleasantness, which the body interprets as danger.

Procrastination is the antithesis of perseverance. It is the avoidance of tasks due to emotional resistance. Procrastinators often try to convince themselves that putting things off can yield productivity in other areas. However, the fact remains: procrastination comes about because of distaste for a task, which itself stems from fear. To procrastinate means to allow negative stress to further invade the body, in the form of guilt, pressure and self-deception. Stress causes damage wherever it goes. Procrastination is not a disease *per se*, but it is an illness of the spirit. It invites poor choices that turn into unhealthy habits that swallow time and strangle opportunity.

Identify your goals and make plans to reach them: As a neurologist and a Holocaust survivor, Viktor Frankl once said, "Life can be pulled by goals just as surely as it can be pushed by drives." Goals are like magnets, the bigger they are, the stronger their pull.

I come across many people who ask me how I keep myself in such good shape. They tell me they want to lose weight, but how they cannot. They complain that they have no time, and besides, "it would take too long to reach my goal." That's classic. A person fears the change, the hardship and the uncertainty of a weight loss program. Emotionally, this is an unpleasant thing – a threat. Then they rationalize: no time, too many months. That's the one-two punch of the body's emotion-logic equation. Anything that is feared by the dominant emotional side of the brain can be translated into logical justifications by the rational side. This leads to procrastination or worse, outright quitting.

No matter what story or circumstances I hear from people, I always offer the same advice: make small changes. A person wishing to lose weight or get fit does not have to go to a gym for many hours every day. It is better to start slow, maybe setting aside thirty minutes for two to three days a week. Or make simple changes to your routine; take the stairs instead of an elevator; or choose a whole grain snack over a pastry. Habits can take days, weeks or months to become part of a person's life, but once that habit is established, positive change starts to happen almost effortlessly. This is much like rolling a ball down a hill and watching it pick up pace with ease. Set small realistic goals that can be accomplished without threatening that inner emotional defensive self.

Manage your time. I mean really! Manage it! Dealing with tasks and priorities requires action and thought. Technically, of course time cannot be managed at all—time is a constant. It is what you do with the tasks inside of a block of time that makes the difference. Perhaps if more people saw it this way, and called it *task management* instead of *time management*, they would be able to focus more clearly on the solutions.

To succeed in managing tasks, you need to become proactive. You need to anticipate rather than simply react. You need to develop habits and keep them front of your mind. Identify and pool your resources. Before starting a task, make sure you have everything needed to complete the task at hand. This will prevent any unnecessary distractions.

Plan your method: Medical research has shown that when you visualize the process of a task, the job becomes easier. A simple remedy to put this to test is to close your eyes and picture yourself doing the task. Researchers have found that the human brain has an incredible ability to fill any gap in a story that might not really be feasible or true.

To test the theory of false memory, scientists interviewed a group of people who had visited Disneyland and then showed them fake Disneyland advertisements that used Bugs Bunny as the central character. Bugs Bunny is not, of course, a Disney character; he is a product of the Warner Brothers studio. Later during an interview, 40% of the participants claimed they vividly remembered seeing a Bugs Bunny character roaming the Disneyland grounds. They had simply filled this extra fact into their memories.

The brain works fast and sometimes carelessly when storing memories without attending to details. It will eventually fill in the gaps. For example, you may hate being stuck in traffic jams, but can you recall the first time you were ever stuck in one? It is difficult because the brain spreads memories into general lessons that it can reuse later. Think, for example, about the last thirty minute conversation you had with someone. Most people are not able to recall everything that was said during the conversation of that length; instead the mind will make important mental notes. That is why you may be able to remember the highlights of the conversation rather than word for word.

The successful completion of tasks and the attainment of goals can be strenuous, but as football coach Lou Holtz said, "It's not the load that breaks our back; it's how we carry it." A sound method always wins.

Plan for distractions: There will always be a text message you must attend to, or a call you need to take. These new stimuli distract the mind, since the mind forms part of the human nervous system, which itself is hard-wired to respond to new information.

The art of managing time, then, must include the ability to set you apart from the false urgency of these messages or handle them without losing momentum. When it is truly necessary to attend to a call or answer a colleague, try taking 30 seconds to bookmark or record the thought or idea. Otherwise it will be forgotten.

Plan for failure: When you fail to plan, you are actually planning to fail. This is a central rule understood by project managers and engineers. We can certainly benefit from understanding this rule as well; to get things done in a timely manner, we must have a plan. Without planning, failure is inevitable. But with a plan in hand, failure or partial failure can be mitigated or lessened. You have back up plans or contingencies. Failure is an event—it is never a person. As such, events and activities can both be planned for and learned from. As a favorite professor of mine once said, "*Failure prepares the way for success.*"

From perseverance comes experience, and from experience comes that lifelong body of knowledge called **wisdom**...

5

Wisdom

Feed opportunities and starve problems | Peter Drucker

I often asked my grandfather to allow me to look at his diary, which he kept very dear to his heart. I would often ask what he wrote and why he wrote so often. Was it interesting gossip? Poetry? A record he kept of the people who owed him money? My curiosity filled me with a strong urge to look into his diary, and I would have done so if he hadn't kept it under his pillow. I once insisted that he give me a clue about what it was or at least teach me a few of the things he had written. After much nagging, he finally sat me down and said, "What I have in here are words that you can rewrite by making the right decisions in life." At the age of eleven I was not fully able to understand what he meant by that, but his words comforted me. I was happy to know that I too could one day have a diary of my own.

Wisdom is a part of character, and just like character, it is not something we are born with. Nor is it something that can be purchased. Wisdom can only be *earned* through the years. There are many ways by which a person can achieve wisdom, but the most essential component is *giving*.

I once participated in an exercise that was conducted in Psychology seminar, in which a word is spoken, and the participant is given three seconds to respond with a name of a well-known person. The idea behind this exercise is that the people named represent the type of people the participants aspire to become. When the word "wise" was presented, the results were astonishing. There were some peculiar choices such as Hugh Hefner, but a vast majority chose Isaac Newton, Albert Einstein, Thomas Edison, Nelson Mandela, and Dr. Martin Luther King, all of whom were selfless role models who served humanity. It was a subconscious declaration by the participants who identified that true wisdom lies in helping others. The act of giving and the act of receiving are both acts of need. At one end of the spectrum a wise person fulfills a need to share by giving selflessly, while at the other end, a person in need receives it, as part of the act of mercy.

People expect to receive wisdom through education. Education is undoubtedly a major contributor to knowledge, but true wisdom lies within. Many call it intuition, but it is in fact wisdom.

Medical practitioners work in an environment in which there are rules and regulations that guide behavior. This heavily regulated way of practicing medicine can sometimes prove demoralizing. Too often, for example, doctor's request excessive laboratory and radiologic testing to simply avert litigation. Corporations create rules to enhance workflow and ensure user safety. Such limitations rob people of intuitive wisdom. There comes a time, in any type of profession, when stringent rules and procedures force people to stop caring about their jobs, and mediocrity is the end result.

I once took up a tutoring job at a local tutoring center. It was one of the happiest days of my life because I knew I was going to teach kids some of the lessons that I had learned the hard way. These were lessons I had learned in school, work, and life. I was excited for those little fourth grade students, and those kids certainly did not disappoint. They were excited about having a motivated tutor who took extra time to go over concepts that were not clear.

The more effort I would put in, the more these children responded. I was named tutor of the month two consecutive times, and I received bonuses along with awards. It was the best time I had working any job. But then, during the winter, six months into the job, new management took over. They were even more cooperative than the previous administrators. They cared very much for children and showed full-hearted effort in making learning an experience rather than a task. They often brought in guest speakers to talk to the children about their future. This new management really knew what they were doing when it came to motivating young minds. However, the new management spent so much on students that they did not offer any incentives for the tutors, and soon, one by one the existing tutors left and others took their place.

The problem here is that in our society we over-incentivize everything. This practice robs people of the desire to simply do the right thing, which should be its own reward. Instead, gain comes first. In this case the tutors had less interest in teaching the kids, who represent the future of our country, than they did for their own materialistic goals. When these materialistic needs weren't satisfied, they walked. These tutors just kept coming and leaving because they saw that management was more interested in investing in new methods of teaching than they were in over-filling the pockets of the teachers. This frequent turn over can be catastrophic for any institution or the people that work with that system.

Incentives, therefore, may rob people of the true appreciation of work. In places where incentives are the only driving force, mediocrity soon follows. Now do not get me wrong, we all need to earn for a living, but what good is it if integrity and following the path of your heart are compromised solely by avarice?

Wisdom is peace. Wisdom is happiness. Wisdom is within us, and it helps us use our intuitions to make the right call no matter what the circumstances are. Sure people may bend the rules, but it is better when rules are bent not for personal gains, but rather for those in need of help. Take for example playing catch. No-one needs a rulebook since the process of catching and throwing a ball is natural. The feel for the ball makes catching and throwing mentally effortless. Similarly, people generally do not – or should not – need rules and regulations or any other guideline to say what is right. It is the feel for what is right that should guide people through life.

In this current fast-paced society people seem to have more tasks to do and not enough time to do them. This often leads to the need to make decisions on the fly, leading to regret. If this habit is not addressed, then this type of knee-jerk reaction becomes a person's identity, leading them down a path in the opposite direction of the attainment of wisdom.

I remember the last time my cousin Ed visited me. I had not seen him for two years since he and his family moved to Texas. Ed is a six-foot-tall, 300-pound teddy bear. However he struggles to accept any talk that would motivate him to get back in shape. Everyone in the family was aware of his sensitivity towards his weight, and we were all careful to show our support for him and his weight loss goals in the most caring way possible. So it came as a shock and a challenge when my six-year-old nephew came straight out and told him that he was fat.

It is important to pause for a minute and think about how anyone would respond to this.

Ed was furious. He exploded with rage and cursed and yelled at my nephew, which sent my nephew running to his mom out of fear. Was Ed's angry reaction justified? Probably not! Ed meant no harm; he simply reacted towards my nephew in just the same way he would to anyone who criticized him. However, perhaps a wiser reaction for him here would have been to assess the situation and to understand how his anger would affect the psyche of a child.

Perhaps a good way to approach this situation would have been to simply embrace the criticism and say "You know what, you are right. I really try hard to lose weight, because I want to be in shape just like you are. Come sit next to me and tell me your secret." This approach not only would have given Ed the chance to diffuse his own frustrations about his weight, but it would have also made my nephew empathetic about other people's struggles. Children have an incredible ability to learn and feel things that adults often shield themselves from. By having a wiser approach, he could have avoided the dangers that anger brings, and could perhaps have opened up a few learning channels.

As adults we interact successfully with others by following social norms. Subtlety and tact, for example, help diffuse negative reactions and spare feelings while still getting a point across. Lots of things must be considered if we decide to be blunt instead. Children, though, do not know these boundaries and they will often say things we would least like to hear; the things others might be afraid to mention.

Knowing and analyzing things rather than just reacting is the source of real power. Being sincere and truthful is the greatest homage we can pay to truth. In the words of Socrates, "*The way to gain a good reputation is to endeavor to be what you desire to appear.*"

Wisdom comes as a comforting sage when dealing with uncertainties, such as the **fear** of failure...

6

Fear

Always do what you are afraid to do | Ralph Waldo Emerson

Fear rules people—it is the single strongest motivator within the human body. This is a good thing in one sense, as it helps keep you alive. The fear of dangerous situations allows us to avoid them either through instinct/reflex or through conscious thought. But fear can also hinder progress by making people avoid opportunities, procrastinate or approach situations in the wrong way.

Fear is best handled by converting thoughts into facts; moving from emotion to logic; from vague awareness to a plan of action. Lets observe fear in the various ways it presents itself.

Fear of Failure

You may find yourself afraid of trying something new simply because you fear you might not succeed. Fear of failure is terrifying and debilitating, and has been magnified through the observational lens of society. To maintain a specific personal image, the ego forbids people from trying anything that might bring criticism or ridicule from the outside world. We convince ourselves that everyone will judge us if we fail, but somehow we will not be judged if we never try anything at all. However, no matter what socioeconomic class anyone belongs to, there will always be criticism and friction at every turn. This is the nature of life. Criticism is like the motor oil of the car; it is a necessary lubricant. Failure is only a state of mind, and it can be dealt with using the abilities we already possess.

We all have the ability to cultivate a winning attitude. Both death and fear have finality to them. One takes away life, the other takes away opportunity. The main difference between death and fear is that death only kills once and often without our knowledge, but fear kills over and over again.

Fear of Calamity

Our minds are bombarded daily by advertisements and news-feeds that impact social behavior. Over the last decade, terrorism and domestic violence have been featured regularly in the headlines, and consequently the media has convinced us we should be afraid of these catastrophes because they lurk just around the corner. However, any statistician will admit that this is simply not true. Natural deaths vastly outweigh deaths caused by dramatic events, but since natural deaths are not interesting, they do not make the headlines. As a result, we tend to ignore the real culprits, not be-cause we are ignorant, but because the human spirit resolves with the inevitable outcomes of life by continuing to move forward.

Fear of Financial Ruin

We all need money to live, but most people do not have enough. Not because everyone is unemployed, but because those who are lucky enough to have cash flow find themselves drowning in debt through poor financial choices. There is actually an acronym that states that the word "job" actually stands for "**j**ust **o**ver **b**roke," since most people spend more than they make and then spend a lifetime trying to catch up. The fear of financial ruin goes hand-in-hand with the fear of owning up to reality: to truly assess just how deeply in debt a person is, or just how little money they have left, is threaten-ing and depressing. Fear tells us to avoid such confrontations, and stay instead in a comfortable world of avoidance and denial.

Fear of Ill Health

How many people do you know who avoid going to the doctor or dentist out of fear? Maybe it's the fear of the cost of a visit, maybe it's fear of what they will learn, or a powerful combination of both. We become fatalistic, feeling that whatever happens will happen, and that fate has a stronger hold over us than being proactive.

Fear of Love and Friendship

You may go out of your way to avoid becoming emotionally intimate with others. Whether on the level of friendship, or on the level of love, there are many people who fear *discovery*. Are you afraid that someone will find out that you are not as wonderful, smart or successful as first impressions might have conveyed? This may be what causes some to avoid closeness, thereby losing all of its benefits.

Fear is a dominant negative motivator opposite to optimism. While both of these motivational forces lead to an ultimate destination, fear makes us relive past experiences of failure. It motivates by conjuring up, unpleasant feelings such as, disappointment and a fear nothing will change and that past experiences will only repeat themselves. It projects these ideas into the future, condemning all new ideas and initiatives to the same fate.

Fear can be beaten

The good news is that fear can be beaten— as it cannot stand up to knowledge and action.

One of the best ways to put fear in its place is to put all the facts on the table. Whatever the news is, once it has been given a name, it can be grasped and taken on. *Talk replaces thought.* Talking to a friend, a mentor, a professional advisor – these are all methods you can use to discard vague, shapeless fears out of your mind and replace them with solid, identifiable objects.

Words replace ideas. Writing thoughts, worries, fears and other negatives down on paper also allow them to take shape. Once you can see it, you can work with it.

Self-determination keeps fear at bay

Self-determination and self-control are qualities that keep fear at bay. Rather than blaming someone else for a failure, if we have a sense of self-determination and self-control, we can look in the mirror, and take personal responsibility for our own future. Success comes with a willingness to take risks, and a willingness to fail while doing so. It is impossible to gain the fruitful prizes of life without taking any risks. As Thomas Jefferson once said, "*To gain something you have never had, you must be willing to do things you have never done.*" According to him, life requires initiative. Since we do not always know when the sun may shine, we must keep all our doors and windows open. The walls that we build around us to keep our disappointments at bay also tend to keep out opportunity.

Often – very often, the greater person is the one who can put the interests of others before him or herself and make **sacrifices**…

7

Sacrifice

Dreams do come true if we only wish hard enough. You can have any-thing in life if you will sacrifice everything else for it. | Sir J.M. Barrie

I once heard a story about a group of three best friends who had been friends since kindergarten. As kids they would go to school together, sit next to each other on the school bus and also in class. They had sleepovers, did their homework together and played to-gether. They lived like this for all the years of their youth, and they remained friends even as they became adults and their lives began to take shape independently. Two of the three friends turned out to have average lives: they had average houses, cars, and average jobs. The third friend, however, became extremely wealthy. He lived a lavish life. He was the CEO of a multimillion-dollar food company. He drove luxurious cars, ate in fancy restaurants, mar-ried a beautiful woman who he dearly loved and with whom he had a very happy marriage. His success always baffled the other two friends. They never understood how he became so rich, but they were too embarrassed to ask him.

The friends were invited to a private party at which their million-aire friend was celebrating a new contract his company had just been given. He announced that the new deal had the potential of transforming his company into a Fortune 500 company. It was a momentous achievement that deserved a celebration.

As the evening wore on, the two friends built up the courage to finally ask the question that they had always wanted to ask. "Tell us John," they said. How did you become so wealthy? We have known you since childhood. We all grew up together. We went to the same school, we all had same friends, and we all shared the same hobbies. What made you stand out? How come you have everything and we don't?" In response John smiled and said, "Let me share with you the secret of my success. Do you guys remember when I decided to go away for work, while you guys stayed back here with your families and children?" They replied, "Yes, of course we remember. You left your wife, kids, and friends for nearly five long years, all in search for a better living. However, you returned with nothing. In fact we lent you money to return home."

John looked at the two and nodded as if to acknowledge their true friendship. He then went on to say, "I am grateful to you guys for being there when I needed you two the most, but you see, you have misunderstood the important lesson here. While I was away from my family and all that I hold dear to my heart, I worked hard to make my dreams come true. Somehow, the hard work just wasn't enough. I was still not able to make ends meet. Then one day at a birthday party, my colleague introduced me to a very rich man who was a true class act. We spoke about various subjects and I knew he liked my enthusiasm. I knew I impressed him during our conversation on business leadership skills. As we reached the end of our conversation, he invited me over for lunch. I was excited and could not sleep the night before. The next day we had a great conversation, it was finally then that I decided to ask him about his wealth. I asked how I too could become wealthy. He asked, 'How bad do you want it?' I said, 'Real bad.' He paused to take a final sip from his cup, and suggested we should go for a swim, and to this I agreed."

John continued, "What was to follow, I could not have imagined in my wildest dreams. At the end of the swim, as I made my way out of the pool, the wealthy man pushed my head under water and held me as I struggled for breath. I soon felt as if death was inevitable. After a few seconds of this, he quickly pulled me out of the water. I came out gasping for breath. He tossed me a towel and asked me to meet him at the coffee table as he walked away. I pulled myself together not understanding what had just happened. Back at the coffee table, before I could ask why he did what he did, he asked me in a very calm tone, 'What were you thinking while I held you underwater?' I replied, 'I was desperate for air, I felt like I was going to die if I didn't get any air!' He said 'well then, you have learned the secret to success.' 'What do you mean?' I said. 'Well,' he replied, 'if your need for success is equivalent to your need for oxygen, then I assure you, that you will achieve success.'"

Looking at his two friends, John continued, "It was then that I understood how to achieve my dreams. I knew the lesson I had just learned was the wisest thing anyone had ever taught me. I knew that if I wanted to succeed in life, I had to work around the clock and dedicate myself mentally to that task. You see guys, if it was not for the sacrifice I made to leave everything I love behind, I would not have learned the greatest lesson of my life."

Sacrifices come in all shapes and sizes. Some people sacrifice personal happiness to ensure the well-being of others, many do it for financial security, and some sacrifice in the name of their faith. In the story above, John was not the only one who sacrificed; his wife and children did, too. An act of sacrifice is seen by many as a divine act that brings one's inner heaven one step closer, since no act is as charitable or favorable as the act of sacrifice.

- To get a good grade on an exam, you must sacrifice free time and give it over to study.

- To succeed in a marriage, you must dedicate time to commitment with spouse and family, to the point at which your spouse's happiness becomes more important.

- To succeed in a friendship, you must learn to be sincere, sacrificing mercenary thoughts for honesty and openness.
- To succeed in obtaining a job promotion, you must learn to work for the company and not just for the paycheck.

In all of these circumstances, there is an obligation to give with no expectations attached.

Freeing yourself from the slavery of your negative thoughts means sacrificing old thoughts in the name of new prosperous ones. Today, in our high-speed world, it can be difficult to take the time to think and plan. In fact, people have so little time to strategize that the idea of making a personal sacrifice in the name of advancement seldom occurs. All positive change, however, has to start from within, and when you make the conscious decision to make a change, any personal obstacle can be conquered.

Sacrifice, then, means to offer something of yourself, in order to do better for yourself and others. It is an internal action. There is also another way to do better for yourself and for others, an external method, called **communication**...

8

Communication

Communication is a skill that you can learn. It's like riding a bicycle or typing. If you're willing to work at it, you can rapidly improve the quality of every part of your life. | Brian Tracy

Communication is often overlooked as a key component of prosperity. Any successful leader, when asked about the path to success, will always mention communication. Communication is the foundation on which success is built. Of course, hard work and persistence are necessary as well, but when you do not communicate ideas or thoughts effectively, the result is wasted effort. Job promotions, for example, do not come easily when ideas and thoughts are not shared. The quality of our life is reflected in the quality of our communication, and good communication serves two basic functions; it educates and liberates.

More often than not, you do not get to the top by your own efforts alone. Many aspects come into play, including a willingness to collaborate with others by maximizing communication channels. It is also important to know how to, delegate work and become time-efficient.

You communicate everyday with those who share your life—your spouse, kids and friends because you understand the importance of staying in touch and that any bond is only as strong as your word. Take, for example, the old cliché, "*Honey I am home!*" Why is it so important to convey this fact? Could it possibly be an appreciation for the patience and hard work the spouse puts into managing the house? Is it because we are glad to be back amid the comfort of the family? Could it mean that we are home and are willing to share the responsibilities and tasks of the household? What message are we sending when we communicate in this way? Anyone with a strong understanding of communication would emphasize that when we communicate well, half of the task – no matter how big or small – is already completed.

I remember one time when I went to a family barbecue, where I met David, an old college friend who I had not seen in a few years. I remember during those college days he would always talk about how he resented his father, who they did not get along because of their differences of opinion. David felt as if his father had never wanted him as a son. There was a period in his life when his father did not speak to him for over a year as David had refused to go back to college. David's father walked with a limp and would often ask his daughters to bring him whatever he needed, but when they were absent, instead of asking David for help, he would quietly and painfully go and get what he needed. All this time David felt his father's resentment.

During my conversation with David, we recalled old times and cherished a few past moments before walking over to the dinner table. At the table, David introduced me to his father as he sat by his father's side fixing him dinner.

"Mr. Haddad," I said, "how is work?"

"Very well," he said, with affirmation. "David has taken over my restaurants and has totally turned around the family fortune."

As I looked at David he had a smile across his face as if to say, "Your praises are far too kind, but thank you for recognizing me in front of a friend." Mr. Haddad continued, "I remember not having enough time for my kids and my grandchildren, but now that David's taken over our financial situation, I get to go places with my grandkids and my wife; places I did not know existed."

As the night went on, we had various conversations over various subjects, and whenever Mr. Haddad found the chance to praise David, he did. It was as if the two were friends, just like David and I.

Afterwards I pulled David aside to seek an explanation for the contradiction in his past stories and his father's behavior today. I asked, "What has changed since the last time we met, when you would refuse to go home until after your father had gone to sleep? Tell me, what did you do to turn all this around?"

David smiled and said, "I have not changed anything, except for one basic thing that kept me in the dark for a very long time and clouded my judgment." He said as hard as it was for him to face all the difficulties that he was having at home, he understood that change was needed. So, he finally decided to take his mother's advice and made the attempt to communicate with his father. "The rest was history," he said. "All this time I was under the impression that my father had abandoned me, but after we started talking, we each expressed what we felt, and finally I understood that my father was not upset with me because I did not want to go back to college. Rather he just wanted me to accept and share responsibility at home and at work. I was able to tell my father that I wanted to look after him and my mother. I have since taken over my father's restaurant business, and since I wanted to succeed in our family business, I went back to college to get my Masters in Business Administration."

David's story is a true testament to the power of communication.

Sharing bright and productive ideas or thoughts starts a ripple effect resulting in creative synergy. When we communicate, we absorb the energy and identity of others to create solutions and ideas that could not have happened in isolation. Ideas are only as powerful and as resourceful as the number of people they reach. Communication reminds us that there are others out there striving to be happy and prosper just like us – people we can talk to, relate to, share with, and learn from.

Effective communication starts from the inside out and not the other way around. We must first learn to clear our own conscience and understand that our greatest assets are those around us. Even when others have unfavorable opinions about us, for whatever reason, this should not change the fact that we can still like them. This is the first step to effective communication. Our attitude can shape and change the world around us. If we are stuck in a hostile environment, we can change things around simply by communicating nothing but compassion in return. No-one will care much about the worth or ideas of another person, until they figure out how much they are cared for in return. For example, it is always better to respond to an angry or a hateful comment with one filled with compassion. Rather than putting someone in their place, it is better to put yourself in their place in order to figure out what it is that troubles them. This is one of the qualities of a great leader. It is not just the cards you hold—it's the way you play a poor hand well that sets you apart.

I have had the great fortune of travelling to many places around the world and meeting all sorts of interesting people with different backgrounds and nationalities. Two of my most memorable trips were to Dubai and Venice. While both cities were breathtaking in their own right, my most memorable moment came while we were sailing on the Grand Canal in Venice. Our gondolier "Luigi" spoke elegantly about the history of the Venetian culture, I listened, as the charm and the beauty of all the sights we were seeing moved me. The gondolier, a man in his late fifties, sang as he rowed the boat swiftly through the canal, showing his effortless rowing strokes. After listening to him singing *Sul Mare Luccica (Sanata Lucia)* I asked him to tell me more about the people of his city. I felt I would like to move out here someday and I wanted to know how the people here take to the newcomers.

"Sure," he said, "But please answer this question—where you come from, how do the people take to new people in town?"

I said, "Well, where I come from, people are busy and barely have the time to help. In fact many are rude." Luigi the gondolier said, "Well that's just too bad. I guess you will have to settle elsewhere because the folks out here are no different." It was déjà vu all over again, because I had experienced this very same response in Dubai.

A year earlier, a few friends and I had planned a trip to visit Dubai to witness the fireworks ringing in the New Year. Dubai did not disappoint. A spectacular show of fireworks draped the *Burj Khalifa* - the tallest building in the world - in a way that captured the imagination. The shimmering fireworks painted the colors of the UAE flag across the sky, while the appreciative crowd took pictures and danced. Everyone felt this was truly a once in a lifetime experience. The following day, while visiting the Dubai museum, I met a gentleman from Ireland. He and I fancied the beautiful *Al-Fahidi* Fort. After chatting about our native backgrounds and families, I asked him about Ireland and told me I would love to visit. I expressed my desire to visit the Boyne Valley, Ring of Kerry, the famous cliffs of Moher, and the Aran Islands. He told me that truly these places were one of a kind. So then I asked him about how the people were out there. As a seasoned traveler with over thirty-five countries seen, he said, "They are just like the folks back at home. But when you open yourself up, the world is your playground." He was diplomatic in his deliverance of a very important message that I heard echoing in Luigi's words. The lesson was simple, "It is not where you are, but what you are inside that should help you find your inner peace." Zig Ziglar phrased it well when he said, *"If you go out looking for friends, you're going to find they are very scarce. If you go out to be a friend, you'll find them everywhere."*

In both of these stories the message is clear. If you address the inner conflicts, the external point of view will take care of itself.

There is an old cliché that says, *fool me once; shame on you, fool me twice; shame on me*. I had let my inner conflict fool me twice, and if it hadn't been my willingness to communicate the foolish ideology I had been telling myself, Luigi would not have been able to show me a new path, and quite frankly if had it not been for Luigi, I would have probably been fooled for the third time.

Effective communication also brings out the good in people. This is the focus of 50 scientific studies funded through The Institute for Research on Unlimited Love, headed by Stephen G. Post, PhD, a professor of bioethics at Case Western Reserve University School of Medicine. This investigation of compassion and kindness showed that nine out of ten people would prefer to do good for others.[1] Communication is definitely the platform through which these people can fulfill their noble desires. However, throughout my years of traveling and communicating with people from all over the world, there are really only two very specific characters that seem to exist wherever I go: the enigmatic character and the social charismatic character.

The enigmatic character tends to be more of an introvert, and whenever I see such a person, an imaginary alarm goes off in my head. I think of all of the magical power this person is truly missing out on. The charismatic character, on the hand, has a great deal of that power. Here is an example of such a charismatic person:

I was on vacation from school and was excited to enjoy a nice long summer break. My father, however, had other plans. He would wake me up early in the morning for prayers and then usher me out the door for a two-mile jog, all in the name of discipline. According to my father, luck was a salesman who only did business with those who were truly worth his time. I could not understand his philosophy back then, but I knew he had gotten it from his own father.

This routine went on for a few days: I would run then spend the day reading. Finally, I said to myself, "This is no way to spend my summer vacation, I need to get a job that will keep me busy until my friends are free in the afternoon." So I took a job working in a local bakery working for Frank. He owned the bakery and was well thought of in our town.

I cannot think of a more charismatic man than Frank. He knew the names of all of his customers and would often chat with them about their kids and family and always mentioned the name of each family member. Frank started his business by baking cookies and selling them from his house. He graduated to selling cookies out of his truck, and was then able to open his own store, all in less than two years. His demeanor with his employees was no different; he knew all there was to know about them. I knew I liked working for Frank because we often spoke about my favorite sports team. The other employees also loved working for Frank. He knew what they liked and what they disliked. I always wondered how he did it.

I tried imitating Frank on several occasions, but the size of crowd I attracted was similar to the size of crowd that cheered me during free throw practices in my backyard – in other words, none. Frank was a heavyweight when it came to working a crowd! Like a boxer that unleashes flurries of punches, Frank unleashed humor in a similar manner. Like a boxing match which drew oh's and ah's from the crowd, Frank drew laughter and cheers. He gave wise advice to anyone who came to him for help. Everyone thought Frank had some sort of a business degree that helped him excel in his business ventures.

It was only years later, after being away because of school and work, I finally caught up with Frank one day and we talked. Frank insisted that I tell him all about my education and what I had been doing. After I told him my story, Frank told me about how his business had expanded from one store to seven stores. I said, "Well then I am guessing you are not working around the clock anymore. You must be enjoying life now."

Frank laughed. "Are you kidding me?" he said. "Where else can I go to meet such wonderful people who inspire me with their everyday stories that have helped me learn about business?" I said, "But Frank, you do not need any tips in business! You have always had a good understanding of business." Looking at me as if I was crazy, Frank said, "I built up my first store on hard work and with a little bit of luck on my side. My other six stores came from meeting some brilliant people who invited me into their lives and taught me the fundamental of success."

I said, "Frank, where did you meet these people?" He said, "I guess I attracted them to my store by word of mouth." Speaking of word of mouth I said, "I know you are great with words Frank, and I think I am finally ready to ask you the big question. Tell me, how do you do it? What is the key to your success? Why is it that while the rest of us come to the batting mound hoping we do not strike out, you come out thinking how to top the range of your previous home run?"

To this Frank replied, "It's pretty simple if you understand your own anatomy."

"What do you mean?" I said.

Frank, who has no college degree, let alone a high school education said, "God has given us two ears and one mouth. Therefore, we should listen more than we talk."

I knew right that moment that Frank spoke about a very important skill of communication, specifically the skill of listening.

To this I said, "Wait just a minute Frank. You talk way more than you listen. In fact you talk when people do not want to talk. You talk when people are in a good mood or a bad mood. You talk to everyone. You talk about sports, cultures, food, religion; you talk about families, friends, relatives, pets; you talk politics, socioeconomic statuses, taxes and you certainly never miss the chance to cheer someone up by offering a free snack."

I went on and on recounting all of the things he did, and how he was a superstar in his own league. Frank couldn't help but smile throughout my protest about him being an excellent speaker but not much of a listener. Then Frank finally said, "You see what I mean? I always listen more than I talk."

It hit me then that Frank was right on the money. Throughout all the years that I knew him, I realized that I had done most of the talking. During my time working for Frank, he would ask simple basic questions about my liking, and then once he found out what sport I liked, he would want to know what team I liked. Once he knew that, he would ask about the player I liked the most. These simple basic questions helped Frank understand how to get the most out of me while keeping me engaged in the business, not as an employee, but rather as a baker. He called his staff *bakers* and not *employees*.

It was then that Franked revealed his primary rule for success. He said, "To be successful you must think from other people's perspective before you look at things from your own perspective."

"I don't understand, Frank," I said. "How can I not see things from my perspective? Who cares what the others perspective is? They have their own way of thinking and I have my own. They live under different circumstances than I do. How will their perspective help me solve my problems?"

He said, "If your problems are greater than the world's problems, then you must create your own world and go live in it. But until then, you must learn to live in the one you already live in, and to successfully live in this one you must give way for others, build tolerance, and understand that your painful story just might not be painful enough for the listener. Remember that the planets revolve around the sun and not around you. By putting people first, you have everything to gain and only your empty brain account to lose." He said he sold cookies from his house to the same people every day, and for years this paid him well. However, he knew his true talents needed a bigger stage to perform. He needed to showcase his skills and truly make it to the top. So he moved out and made a one hundred percent effort to talk to people and a two hundred percent effort to listen and take mental notes.

Frank said the idea of exploring other approaches to success came to him one day while he was playing Jenga. This is a board game in which players remove blocks from a stable tower and place them on top of the tower creating an unstable structure. With each turn the tower's chances of collapsing increase. All angles need to be considered in order to become the last player standing (winner). Any shortsighted move can lead to disappointment.

Frank said he juggled with the idea of Jenga and understood that success lies in seeing the bigger picture. Sometimes the right strategy might not be immediately visible, unless the player changes perspective. He went on to say that sometimes patience and the vision to see the broad spectrum of the matter at hand are both needed. He said that he understood from his years of being in the bakery business that the most important force that a man is driven by is his own desires, but he didn't mean that in a negative way.

This became my initial drive to become a better communicator. Over the years I have learned to become compassionate and I have understood that communication is not just a financial asset but also a spiritual one. Frank's way of communicating is truly an exemplary display of how words can move a stone.

Of course, one of the best ways of communicating is to keep it light with a sense of **humor**...

9

Humor

You can turn painful situations around through laughter. If you can find humor in anything, even poverty, you can survive it. | Bill Cosby

Steve is the CEO of a clothing line based in San Francisco, California. During the 2008 recession, while every business was taking a hit, Steve's business flourished. He bought a brand new house that year while others struggled to keep up with their mortgage payments. While the national media covered the overall financial impact of recession, Steve refused to watch any news that would bring his spirits down. Instead he would turn on Comedy Central Channel and just laugh away. All of Steve's employees were just as happy during these hard times.

Steve was a great leader who found joy even in the gloomiest of moments. A local journalist caught up with one of Steve's employees to ask how the company flourished during these difficult financial times. The employee simply answered, "Well, we work for Steve." Wondering what this meant, the journalist spoke to a handful of Steve's employees and their responses were the same. The journalist tried to arrange an interview with Steve, but according to Steve's secretary, Steve was always away on business trips.

Finally one day, the journalist received the much-anticipated call from Steve. During the conversation the two exchanged dates for an interview and shared a few laughs. On the day of the interview, while waiting to be called into Steve's office, the journalist frequently heard laughter coming from a board meeting across the hall. The journalist couldn't help but compare this company with the countless others businesses he had spoken with lately. These people had spoken with heavy hearts while they shared their melancholy business stories. The overall feeling had been downright depressing, almost frantic.

The vibe in this company, though, was different. People seemed to be having a good time. Every LCD monitor in the waiting rooms had some sort of educational program showing. Finally the journalist caught up with Steve, and found him to be a warm and a funny character. After a small chat, Steve was ready for the interview. So the journalist asked a few formal questions and then he asked Steve for the key to his success. "Well," said Steve, "Let me first tell you a personal anecdote to set the stage. My granddaughter was sitting in my lap watching her favorite movie, *Toy Story*. I can't help but admit I really like those characters. Anyway, as we watched, my granddaughter looked restless and so I asked her what was wrong. In her very innocent voice she said, 'Grandpa why do you have wrinkles?' and I said, 'Because God made me a long time ago.' She said 'Did He make me?' and I said, 'He sure did, just recently.' She paused for a few seconds and then said to me, 'He sure is getting better at it now, isn't He?'" The interview had turned into a complete comical talk.

The journalist and Steve shared plenty of entertaining moments from their past, joking and sharing stories. Then Steve finally spoke about his success. "I was on the verge of losing my business a few years back," he confessed. "I read many leadership books and attended seminars on how to manage my business more effectively. I gave control, incentives, and encouraged people to strive for more. Despite all of my efforts, my business plummeted. I was always extremely stressed out and therefore dysfunctional. I could not understand why things were not going my way despite the fact that I was following every advice to the last note. Finally one day my granddaughter, who I call my golden girl, was sitting next to me drawing while a news talk show was on the TV. She said, 'Grandpa why are you always watching this boring and depressing show?' I quickly answered to save face but that question really ran through my mind for couple of days until I realized what was wrong. I realized I was not having any fun. I was worried about business deals and events that had not even taken place yet, but here I was worried about things going wrong. Despite getting compliments for being business savvy, the reason my business was not doing so well was simple: We were under a cloud. I decided to change how I viewed the world. I decided to stop receiving facts from other people's perspective, or more specifically from the media's perspective. Instead of starting my day with morning headlines, I watched Comedy Central. Soon I embraced this change and within a few months my company was back in business. When any of my sales managers came to me with bad news, rather than addressing the problem on hand I would engage them in a fun conversation. In the end they always said, 'Steve let me get back to you about this deal that is not working, I think the party needs to hear what I have in store for them.'"

Steve said, "You see, I do not have to tell anyone in this company anything because they all are well-qualified to figure things out. If there is something we need to address, then we have board meetings. My role in this company is to keep reminding everyone to never stop having fun, even in the most desperate times."

Towards the end of the conversation, Steve quoted Mark Twain and said, *"Against the assault of laughter nothing can stand."* The journalist thanked Steve for his time and the following day wrote a review in the business column on Steve's company. Here is how the review went:

During this recession, while many struggle to hold on to what has been otherwise a challenging time in our nation's economy, there are a few things we can learn from Steve & Partners. Their way of addressing what others might call an impossible situation is reminding us that through humor we can overcome the gloomiest of the situations. How you may ask? The explanation to this question is scientific. The human mind works at optimum levels when there is tranquility in life and the fear of losing is buried. Under great pressure even the best of us can face disappointments. But the resilient company of Steve & Partners understands what the rain is to the soil, a smile is to humanity; the inner serenity it produces is inconceivable.

Steve often tells the story at board meetings and other events about how his golden girl reminded him to look past the worst of the scenarios with a sense of humor. He talks about how engaging people in delightful conversations can help ease frustrations and give way to a clear and conscious mind. In our story, what Steve knew was truly powerful and effective. Steve understood that stress and fear are two paralyzing forces that can arrest personal development at all levels. Despite all of his knowledge on leadership and business, it was not until Steve understood the importance of humor that he became successful. Steve couldn't have put it any better when he said, "The wrinkles on my face are the proof of how I smiled in the face of adversity."

Are there other ways to communicate and connect? Of course! People love to hear good things about themselves...they love to hear **compliments...**

10

The Power of Compliment

Too often we underestimate the power of a touch, a smile, a kind word, a listening ear, an honest compliment, or the smallest act of caring, all of which have the potential to turn a life around. | Leo Buscaglia

Compliments can be the most powerful of motivators, even though little attention is paid to them in daily life and things are often taken for granted. All endeavors whether easy or difficult, small or big become endurable when we show compassion and appreciation. Human psychology may be a complex field overall, but there is some easy-to-read truth in the midst of it. For example, regardless of culture and nationality, you take comfort in belonging to or identifying with certain social or political groups. It's a tribal instinct, and it serves to actually reinforce our individual existence. Most of us now live in a sophisticated world with all the amenities and comforts we desire, but the idea of belonging to a group and taking a stand for self-recognition still drives our personal interaction with the world. Think, for example, of the popularity of social media applications such as Facebook and Twitter. This idea can perhaps be broken down further by answering a simple, basic question. Where would you be without the support of your family?

Human interaction almost always happens in groups that have branched off from a common trunk. For most people, family exists at the core, or trunk. Branching groups can include friends, colleagues, neighbors, clubs, the local gym, and the community we live in. All of these groups help us shape our lives one way or another. Approval from others helps build a layer of protection against feelings of alienation, and also protect against too much self-scrutiny.

Our desire for approval starts in infancy, where as children we ask for constant attention and adults signify approval with smiles, kisses and attention. This desire continues with age, yet it evolves so that the types of attention and approval required change to match a more mature outlook. However, even if the desire for attention is no longer as intense, the value of recognition still stands unmatched.

I consider myself a keen observer of people and behavior; this habit has taught me a very important lesson that truly gives life to the idea that giving compliment is a major contributor to happiness and success. During the last holiday season I went shopping and picked out a nice pair of sunglasses for my mother. I had to stop and contemplate whether I could truly afford such expensive sunglasses and how this purchase would impact my cash for the upcoming month. I considered doing what I usually did for her at this time of year, purchasing a nice bouquet of roses. I hoped she would appreciate them once again this year, as much as she might have appreciated those glasses.

While I was having this debate with myself, a woman walked into the store, with her four-year-old daughter at her side. From the look on her face, the woman looked like she had woken up on the wrong side of the bed. She appeared angry, as if she was already having an unpleasant day. As her young daughter asked her for attention, the woman couldn't help but respond in an angry tone.

Angry people make the worst customers. Rage has ways of destroying inner peace, which has a demoralizing effect on everyone in the immediate area. Anger is the ultimate shutdown button for the human brain and prevents processing or analyzing of information. It acts just the way a virus does on a computer. This woman's actions and words created a negative wave that was felt throughout the store. It felt as if all the positive energy had just been sucked out of the room. This is when Leah, the saleswoman, took control and demonstrated the power of a compliment.

Appearing genuinely calm and poised, Leah approached the angry woman and said, "Hi, how may I be of assistance?" The woman requested that Leah help her try on a few glasses and Leah did just that. The customer went from one choice to another, moving from the expensive products to the cheapest ones, all the while growing frustrated by not being able to find anything she liked.

As I observed the interaction between the customer and Leah, I saw the growing distress in this customer's body language, while Leah remained calm. I could not help but notice the expensive accessories the customer was wearing, and Leah noticed also. She asked the customer, "So what does he do?" The customer looked at Leah and said, "Who?"

"Your husband," Leah replied. "The ring on your finger speaks volumes for his taste, both in women and diamonds – both are very beautiful and elegant."

I was amazed at how skillfully Leah had put together the analogy of beauty between diamonds and her customer, who was now very happy. Immediately her body language improved and she smiled and told Leah that her husband was a lawyer. Leah said, "Well that's great. He sure knows how to attract, treat and keep a beautiful woman." This comment was enough to send the customer into a happy hypnotic trance. The customer now slowly started walking back towards the expensive glasses. Leah said, "Would you like me to take all of the glasses out for you to try on?" and the former angry customer – now a happy one – said, "No, I don't want you to go through all that trouble. Just show me this one." She had chosen the most expensive glasses in the store for herself, as well as two other pairs of sunglasses for her daughter and her husband. While Leah checked out the customer at the cash register, she received praises from her other customers about the wonderful staff this store had, and what a marvelous store it was.

Leah took a volatile situation, one that most of us would want to avoid, and made it spectacular by her attitude and timing. While many would avoid giving the angry customer any compliment at all, Leah understood its true power. She understood that by giving a compliment she was not going to become a subordinate to the customer but the very opposite. When Leah complimented the angry customer she not only took control of the situation, she guided the behavior of the customer.

Without the art of compliment, the crudeness of reality would make life unbearable. It is through compliments that we open the doors for others to become exceptional leaders in their own lives. However no-one can expect to spill the waters of compliment on others without getting some on themselves. Anyone who appears constantly worried about only themselves is like a person who constantly talks about personal wealth: neither has anything to offer. Giving compliments freely helps cultivate success in the lives of others. The old German motto, "What I spent, I had; what I saved, I lost; what I gave, I have" gives us the understanding that through the liberal use of compliments we plant the seeds of a successful society and we all reap personal prosperity.

Dr. Andrews, an exceptional psychologist, was called in for a consultation with a patient (college professor) in his late forties who had been admitted to the hospital for injuries he received in a car accident. Even though his wounds had somewhat healed, the medical staff often found the patient in tears from the pain of his wounds. Doctors could not understand why the patient was in pain despite no medical evidence of an underlying cause. The wounds could not have been the reason for his pain. This is when Dr. Andrews truly showed the power of compliment.

After speaking to the patient for a few minutes, trying to understand the reason why the patient could not overcome the pain, Dr. Andrews discovered that the cause of the pain was not from the patient's injuries; rather it was an emotional conflict that had been brewing for months and was finally pouring out. In other words, the patient was suffering from post-traumatic stress disorder (PTSD).

In his subsequent visits Dr. Andrews got to know the patient well, and he would regularly compliment the patient about his prosperous career, his compassion, his love for others, and all the strong leadership qualities he had shown as a college professor. This process of talking to the patient went on for a few weeks and slowly everyone noticed the patient began to smile again. The pain seemed to have gone and the patient was once again talking and exchanging stories with family members. Later in his explanation of the case, Dr. Andrews pointed out the importance of distracting negative thoughts by focusing on self-value to realize one's own worthiness. He explained that not only for others but when we distract ourselves from harmful thoughts and feelings, our body releases serotonin, a hormone responsible for one's own well-being. The idea he explained was simple, "Focus on the good quality and turn it into a compliment. As you will observe, self-appreciation will soon follow." Giving positive praises can do wonders for others, and these powerful expressions can come in the smallest of packages.

You may wonder about the difference between a compliment and flattery. While complimenting someone can ignite prosperity, flattery can be a harmful symbol of how you are perceived by others. The dictionary defines the word compliment as "a polite expression of praise out of courtesy and respect." Flattery, on the other hand, is described as "excessive and insincere praise, especially given to further one's own interests." It is no surprise, then, that when comparing these two different forms of delivering praise, the balance, in terms of quality tilts towards compliment.

The essential elements that give value to any compliment are honesty and sincerity. Without this, you merely have flattery, which will quickly be interpreted as a form of manipulation and insincerity. With this important rule in mind, let's look at the four simple steps in delivering a meaningful and a powerful compliment:

1. **Know what to say**: The human brain has one billion neurons, each of which forms one thousand connections with other neurons. This amounts to over a trillion connections. In technology parlance, this would add up to more than a million gigabytes of storage space, or three hundred years of continuous television recording. Why is this a big deal? Because people are smart. People pick up on subtle gestures, words and mannerisms. When delivering compliments it is important to refrain from being vague. The brain is designed to absorb complex thoughts and details and the more details that are incorporated into a compliment, the more valuable they become. Parents know to take time to analyze their child's drawing and become very creative and specific in their praise. Similarly, successful leaders understand the mastery of the meaningful compliment by avoiding generalities. They are quick to point out what was done well, knowing that what was not done well will automatically take care of itself. Praise should come with no strings attached.

2. **What to praise**: More often than not, you notice how much attention is being paid to you by the things that are said. Praise, therefore, always acts as an acknowledgement of your efforts and hard work overall.

3. **When to praise**: While compliments are mostly exchanged face-to-face, the impact of the compliment is much

more powerful when actually given in the absence of the person being complimented. Just like bad news, good news also spreads fast, with much greater outcome and a much stronger impact. Think back to a compliment you might have heard someone gave in your absence. How did that make you feel? Would you have appreciated its sincerity just as much if it were face-to-face? This is not to say that face-to-face compliments should never exist; rather the point here is to highlight that both forms of delivery have great power and lasting, positive impact.

4. **Praise everyone, always**: It is easy to compliment the extraordinary efforts, but what about the less accomplished hard work that goes on around us? What about the smaller contributions to a project or to society? These things should be praised also, since great things come in small packages. In her beautiful poem, Kate Buxbaum-Prado writes, "*Compliments given from the heart can turn a pauper to a king/or cause the least gifted with song, to open up their mouths and sing.*"

Compliment and praise build pillars of strength within a person. They are central to building one of the most elusive and rare qualities of individuals, **self-confidence**...

11

Self-Confidence

Begin to weave and god will give you the thread | German proverb

This world has a tendency to accept our own judgment of ourselves. If you choose to exude self-confidence, the world will naturally want to let you succeed. In just the same way in which the rising sun pushes back the darkness and allows existence to flourish, self-confidence delivers the energy and warmth that people need to further their travels in life. Too many people live their lives filled with silent despair, while the few confident people find themselves able to trust their own abilities. These confident people have a belief that with persistence and the right approach, they can go from being ordinary to extraordinary. Self-confident people understand how to make the best of the worst and yet maintain integrity. Even in a state of submission or under overwhelming circumstances, a self-confident person remains graceful and understands there is a bigger picture. They do not sweat the small stuff. Self-confident people believe that worrying about minor things represents precious time wasted; time that could have been invested into becoming more productive. Having self-confidence is not about getting overly high; rather it is the fuel that pushes a person *regardless of the circumstances*. We can gladly pay any price once we sincerely believe in the promise. It is self-doubt that creates a perception of incompetence.

Being confident in one area of your life does not mean that you are automatically confident in all other areas. Rather, you have an understanding of where the confidence lies which allows for the achievement of greater success by translating the same mindset into weaker areas. All the knowledge required for success lies within, but there must be a willingness to explore. It is better to pay attention to our abilities than our needs, because through this process we build confidence.

It is easy to confuse low self-confidence with lack of ability, which is a misconception unfortunately reinforced by our own external support systems. The impact of what our peers think or feel about us can have a very strong effect. This is commonly found during the teenage years when peer pressure guides the major part of the behavior. As we grow older and our thoughts become mature and sophisticated, the nature of peer pressure grows as well. As children we react to the demands of our peers, and as adults we react to the demands of our families and colleagues. But a self-confident person understands how to control internal reactions to external pressures by possessing the knowledge of mind over matter. No matter how difficult the task, the act of staying positive can overcome even the most hideous misery. It is not the size of the person that defines strength; but rather self-recognition.

We may occupy our mind with negative thoughts and assumptions that clearly diminish our drive to overcome obstacles. More than anything, such darkness represents a personal lack of recognizing our own greatness. It is possible to talk ourselves out of negative thoughts; in fact this is the first step in achieving ultimate confidence. Scolding leads to emotional and mental paralysis. However, positive self-talk, combined with visualization of goals will fuel the body and spirit with the energy needed to move forward. This is what athletes do as they gaze at the finish line. They see themselves winning. They see their strengths. They love who they are and what they can still become.

The roots of low self-confidence usually start with the very first time we hear the word, "no." This is because in many cases, the word stands as an obstacle to our desires, and therefore as a threat to our sense of esteem. Far from being one of the shortest words in the English language, "no," it is actually one of the longest, since it carries with it a long tail of negativity. This is the case whether outwardly spoken or merely implied.

As you go down the following list of "no's", notice the first thought that comes to mind when reading the list. How would a self-confident person approach these remarks?

'No! You are not smart enough.'

'No! You are too young.'

'No! You are too old.'

'No! You don't know what you are talking about.'

'No! You don't have the means.'

'No! If you try, you will regret it.'

'No! There is no hope for you.'

'No! You are just not good enough.'

'No! You don't have what it takes.'

While daunting and intimidating, here is how a self-confident person would address these remarks.

Remark: "No! You don't have what it takes - or - "No! You are not smart enough."

Resolution: "Well then, I guess there is room for improvement. After all, the biggest room in any house has room for improvement. Step aside while I roll up my sleeves and get to work."

Remark: "No! You are too young."

Resolution: "I wish someone had told that to the 13-year-old Californian boy who in 2010 was crowned the youngest conqueror of Mount Everest."

Remark: "No! You are too old."

Resolution: "Turbaned Torpedo" ran the 10 km marathon at 101 years-of-age. I don't believe that I am too old to try something new."

Remark: "No! You don't know what you are talking about."

Resolution: "That was the same criticism Albert Einstein heard while working on his theory of relativity, which now serves as the basis of many theories, such as quantum electrodynamics. I guess I am in great company, thanks for the compliment."

Remark: "No! You don't have the means."

Resolution: "Steve Jobs was adopted and later dropped out of college to work on his idea. He didn't have the means, but he did have the idea. Thanks for the reminder."

Remark: "No! If you try, you will regret it."

Resolution: "Would India be a free state if Mahatma Gandhi gave in to the threats of the British forces who opposed the hunger strike? History does teach great lessons."

Remark: "No! There is no hope for you."

Resolution: "Just hold that thought. Let me share with you some encouraging words that Jonathan Swift once said, 'Vision is the art of seeing things invisible.'"

Remark: "No! You are just not good enough."

Resolution: "Let me share this story with you: After working for over three years at a bank, for an ungrateful boss who constantly yelled and laughed at his staff, David received a letter stating he was fired because he was not bringing in business. David knew this was not true. The reason the company had been losing business was because the stringent rules and regulations of the company were not well suited for the current economy; in fact they were outdated. David received word that he just was not good enough. A few weeks later, David took up another job at a different bank and within a short time he went on to become the district manager. David later recalled that when he looked up the word projection in the dictionary, it described *projection* as the unconscious transfer of one's own desires or emotions onto another person. David remembered the condescending words of his former boss, and David felt sorry for the man who had fired him.

No matter what age you are, there still remains time to be great, and time to try to be great, on our own terms and in our own way.

Self-confidence is not arrogance or disrespect. Each of us serves as our own link between our past and our future. The resolutions presented here are the representation of our inner voice that encourage and motivate us in an effort to drive us to achieve success. These are real life stories of people who defy the very existence of self-doubt and demonstrate the courage that lays a foundation for self-confidence. All doubts exist in our minds. Once we cross the barrier that limits our vision of prosperity, self-confidence is there for the taking.

As the mind and body grow with confidence, so there evolves a greater capacity for **personal responsibility**…

12

Personal Responsibility

Some pursue happiness others create it | *Ralph Waldo Emerson*

As children, our ambitions and dreams seem unlimited because we cherish the idea of freedom. And we see no obstacles to it. This applies to freedom of expression, thought or achievement—it's all an individual choice. However, over the years these thoughts become limited, not because opportunities no longer present themselves, but because we lack the ability to see the possibilities that surround us.

Some of us have the tendency to fall into the dreary potholes of complacency and mediocrity, holding on to a false perception that our failures do not lie within us, but that it is the world that somehow is to blame. We look outside ourselves and are quick to point fingers at others as the cause of our current dreadful relationship or failed business venture.

Don't forget—for the one finger that is pointing out, three are pointing back at you! The notion that we are solely the product of our environment is a falsity that many people feed on permanently. Having a blame list is acceptable only if we are number one on that blame list; once we do this whatever follows will not matter. There is no liberty or freedom without personal responsibility. We can only be free as long as we use our given freedom responsibly. We cannot leave the development of our potential to mere chances. We must pursue the idea of growth and knowledge with open minds. Our decisions narrow or widen our opportunities.

As kids we dream about growing up and owning big houses and fancy cars, but as adults we tend to stop dreaming. For many, the idea of failure outweighs the possibility of prosperity. An example of how failure can be confronted and turned around can be seen in the story of Eric and his printing company:

Eric's printing company had been given the task of producing 25,000 brochures for the upcoming mayor's public address to a neighboring city. These brochures informed the attendees about the mayor's ongoing projects in local housing, the new city elementary school, and the highway that would pass through the local town. The mayor strongly supported the highway, as it would greatly improve the city's economy.

Eric's company had finished the printing process and had shipped out the package via regular mail, a few days before the event. The night before the event, Eric received a call from the mayor's secretary to inform him that the brochures had not yet arrived. Eric knew this was a blunder on his company's behalf and somehow it needed to be fixed. He reassured the secretary that the package would be there as promised. After hanging up the phone, Eric and his wife knew that this was a total disaster. He knew he had completely blown it by trying to save money and using regular mail, something he later described as one of the most crucial mistakes in his company's history.

Eric pulled himself together and called in the entire staff. He asked them to work overnight producing what had previously taken more than two weeks to produce. Eric and his entire staff worked tirelessly through the night at a frantic pace to meet the deadline. Just before dawn, Eric himself drove a hundred miles to personally deliver the brochures.

Looking back at it, Eric recalls how he felt responsible for his employees' wellbeing as well as his own by staying in business. Eric knew that as a leader of the company he had obligations that had to be met irrespective of the adverse situation. Eric could have fired a few people and blamed others for the blunder, but he knew that taking responsibility would earn him both the respect and loyalty of his employees and customers.

Egos are easily challenged and bruised when responsibility is at stake. Eric realized that in the future, a wise move would be to clarify the responsibility of each individual prior to starting any project. In this case, if things were to fall apart again, his employees would be better able to take direct responsibility to accomplish specific tasks.

Eric knew the importance of promoting responsibility to eliminate excuse making. In choosing between falling into the rabbit hole of fear and doubt and pointing fingers all the way down, Eric chose to stay above ground and demonstrate to his entire staff that all actions have consequences which in turn impact the company. Eric was consistent in his leadership and embodied his words to assure that his company achieved results. Even though his own internal voice occasionally placed doubt in his head, his result-oriented approach overcame his negative thoughts.

Personal responsibility represents the willingness to accept the importance of standards and then make strenuous efforts to live by those standards. Personal responsibility also means that when we fail to meet expected standards, we do not look around for some factor outside ourselves as the culprit; rather all effort should be made to resolve and overcome any obstacle that denies us the right to live by our own standards.

Once we are capable of attainment through personal responsibility, we are then better enabled to support others with **love**...

13

Love

*I have decided to stick with love. Hate is too great a burden to bear. |
Martin Luther King, Jr.*

History is a judge that time-and-time-again has given the verdict in
favor of love over hate. No feeling is as strong and yet mellow as
the feeling of love. It is the one emotion that we never get enough
of, and the one we never give enough of. Everyone in love cheats to
keep more for themselves and less for others. It makes sense in the
initial stages of course, but if the last seed is consumed, then how
will it be possible to replenish empty vessels? There is no sense in
eating the very last seed and then starving and hoping for a miracle.
Miracles do not simply happen out of the blue, they transpire with
the gracious act of love.

When we plant the seeds of love in our hearts, cultivate them and
tend to them, we grow. We become empowered, confident, and
strong as we realize that we possess all the love we will ever need.
It is up to us to make a conscious choice to be happy and at peace.
And it is up to us to spread this message and help tend each other's
gardens. Love is the swiftest form of inner growth, and it is our
responsibility to nurture this growth. Just like a mother giving her
utmost love to her children, we must do the same for ourselves
and those around us. Where there is a presence of love there is
harmony and balance. Without it there is misunderstanding, hatred,

fear and jealousy, which opens the doors to a perpetual abyss.

True happiness starts within. If you wait for someone else to come along and brighten your day, you might as well keep waiting. Taking the initiative to pursue happiness marks the first sign of self-appreciation and responsibility. Remember, eyes do not see what the heart does not feel. Love enriches the world, deepens emotions, extends the horizons, enhances opportunities, and brightens friendships like the sparks of a candle illuminating our faces. It is the act of love that navigates, directs, and makes our existence meaningful. Through its power we create the identity of our egos; we go from being part of a herd to becoming an individual. Love does not decide what it will embrace; rather we make that decision. But what it does choose is the amount of attractiveness and value of that decision. This is like buying a golden necklace: the more carats that get added, the more attractive and valuable the necklace becomes. Keeping this in mind, it is safe to say that our value lies in the amount of love we give to ourselves.

Love and affection is the center of most religions and spiritual beliefs. Self-love is acknowledged both in secular society and the field of psychology, as a key to personal development and fulfilling personal relationships. The goal here is to treat yourself with greater compassion, acceptance, and kindness. As we develop self-admiration and learn to express ourselves more fully, we begin to enrich both our self-esteem and confidence. In the words of Alan Cohen, "To love yourself right now, just as you are, is to give yourself heaven. Don't wait until you die. If you wait, you die now. If you love, you live now."

Here is a very poignant story, one that I share with friends and colleagues, about love:

While having dinner with his family, Jake received a phone call from Carl, a close friend who called because he was on the verge of making one of the most important decisions of his life. When Jake asked what it was, Carl said, "I think I want a divorce." Jake was shocked and could not believe what he was hearing. For years, Jake had been under the impression that Carl had a great marriage and that both he and his wife were happy. "Did you get into an argument?" Jake said.

"No," said Carl. "My wife and I have a good understanding of things. We hardly argue."

"So then what is it?" asked Jake.

"Well," said Carl, "I just don't have the same feelings for my wife. I met a woman a few months back and I feel drawn to her. Every time I am with her, I feel a spark that I have not felt in years. I am convinced that she and I are meant to be together."

Too often people are caught up in situations in which personal principles are compromised by the inner desires that replace faithfulness and sincerity, which are the true navigators of prosperity. When once entered into matrimony, a man and woman belong exclusively to each other until the moment of its dissolution. Their best interest is to keep their imagination from wandering towards the perceived perfections of other people. Love is not a feeling. It is a decision to do right not only once, but over and over again. You may explore various opportunities to find love on the outside, believing that one person cannot fulfill your inner desires of being wanted. But sometimes the hardest things to believe are the only things worthwhile. To love others is to have faith in others, which means that you hold on to what you once accepted, despite your current change of belief. Our disappointments do not occur unless we are expecting something in return.

Love is not negotiable. It is critical for our physical and emotional well-being. It is a healthy state of mind that treats many ailments including depression. In order to understand what this means, think about how the majority of us get our idea of love from the popular culture. People are infatuated with the idea of being swept off their feet when the right person comes along. These ideas are constantly demonstrated in imagery that promises immediate gratification, and like eating too much chocolate, it eventually sets us up for disappointment.

We often go into denial when our love life does not match a cultural ideal. When this happens, you may try changing each other by any means necessary to live out an improbable reality. You may start pointing out another's sins in the hope that confessing may bring salvation. While confessing your own sins may do this, confessing someone else's sins is called backbiting and does not resolve any situation.

It is easy to get lost in the struggle of maintaining balance between cultural and personal reality. The idea here is to understand the key principal of *limerence*, which is a psychological state of extreme infatuation that delivers instant attraction. The only way this turns into love is through the act of will. Love is a skill acquired over time, and lacking this critical skill can be an act of psychological warfare. There are always differences between two people, and the best solution is to resolve, and not find other ways to make it worse. Just how do we resolve this? The answer lies everywhere if we just listen carefully enough. By shifting our focus from ourselves to other people, we can come to common grounds that may work for everyone.

In the words of Oscar Wilde, "*Every fall into love involves the triumph of hope over self-knowledge. We fall in love hoping that we will not find in the other what we know is in ourselves — all the cowardice, weakness, laziness, dishonesty, compromise and sometimes brute stupidity. We throw a cordon of love around the chosen one, and decide that everything that lies within it will somehow be free of our faults and hence lovable. We locate inside another a perfection that eludes us within ourselves, and through union with the beloved, hope somehow to a precarious faith in the species.*"

In our deepest moments of despair we scrutinize ourselves and ask, "Who are we to be brilliant, gorgeous, talented, and fabulous?" These are the moments that build doubt, mediocrity, and ugliness that pours from the deep within. This is an act of making ourselves small that does not serve us or anyone else for that matter. Too much scrutiny not only deteriorates our personal charisma, it also forms a shield against the act of love. It is an act that sparks insecurity in the immediate radius around us, causing a ripple effect on those around us. We can all learn the skill of love by becoming self-generating beings that illuminate the lives of those we care for. Think of an electric generator providing light to all the houses in its vicinity. When we generate love within, everything within our vicinity lightens up and suddenly it becomes a chain reaction. Learning to love others and ourselves is a liberating feeling that shows the way to the less fortunate.

Through the strong forces of love we can help demolish the walls of ignorance and blow away the thick fog of hatred and segregation. The true nature of a person is the desire to help one another. We aspire to live by each other's happiness and not by each other's misery. There is plenty on this earth to go around for everyone. Yet at times we lose our ways in the face of greed and hatred.

With our current knowledge of technology and the world's resources, we have become the most powerful people in the history of mankind. But this knowledge has made us ignorant in many ways, and our cleverness has made us hard and unkind. We think too much and feel too little. More than war, we need peace. As a human race, our greatest inventions have not come in our time of despair, but rather in our time of peace.

But the wars we wage are not all out on the battlefields. There is also an inner war that strives to defeat our positive qualities and replace them with negative emotions such as hate, greed, doubt, intolerance, and resentment. These are the emotions that drill us and treat us like cattle. We all have the potential for goodness. We all have love in our hearts. Hatred consumes all energy in return for mere pennies, whereas love consumes little and returns much.

Love helps people escape the slavery of judgmental thoughts; it liberates our minds to accommodate prosperous thoughts that lead to an eternal spring. We all have the power to make our lives beautiful and to make our lives the greatest adventure. With the power of love in our hearts we can all unite to become a free world, a decent world that holds hope for the unprivileged, the sick and the old. With the power of love we can control and even get rid of the negatives that work against us, and free the positives that can work for us. The hope for us is to become one for the sake of a world of reason, we can all do our part. We can all learn to love.

And love warms the whole body. It is an essential ingredient to sound mental and physical **health**...

14

Health

To keep the body in good health is a duty; otherwise we shall not be able to keep our mind strong and clear. | Buddha

The World Health Organization defines health as "a state of complete physical, mental and social well-being and not merely the absence of disease or infirmity." Health is our resource for everyday life and not the objective of living. While many believe that health simply means eating right and exercising, it is much more than that. Health exists in two different states: physical health and mental health. Neither takes precedence over the other. They are both just as important as our body's need for oxygen and food. Without both, survival is not possible.

Physical health is an important tool for all of us. Populations that experience improved nutrition, health care, standards of living and quality of life generally have abundance in quality of life and longevity. Good health allows us to become better equipped to take on strenuous physical and mental activities.

Physical well-being is something almost anyone can achieve through the development and practice of a healthy lifestyle. This is reflected in our cardiorespiratory endurance, muscular strength, flexibility, and body composition. For our physical wellbeing, it is important to include proper nutrition, and body weight management. It is also important that we abstain from drug and alcohol abuse; practice responsible sexual behavior and hygiene, and to get the right amount of sleep. Too often people find it difficult to commit themselves to exercising because they would rather sit and eat. To such a thought Henry Miller would say, "Our own physical body possesses a wisdom which we who inhabit the body lack. We give it orders which make no sense."

Take the example of Steve S., for example:

Six months after joining the gym, Steve felt frustrated and demotivated. He felt he had not achieved the results that he desired. Despite his trainer's insistence that his hard work had resulted in tremendous improvement, and that he was well on his way to achieving the goals he had set for himself, Steve was not convinced and he thought to himself that it just was not meant to be. He started to show a lack of effort and desire. Steve's trainer knew that this was going to be a problem—one that Steve needed to deal with now before quitting became the only desirable option. One day when both Steve and his trainer were working out, the two shared their stories about their desired outcomes and how they would like to see themselves in the future. The trainer went first and said, "I am satisfied with the way I look. I work hard and I am happy with the results." Steve however, spoke about the posters of bodybuilders he had placed on the walls of his room. He explained how they had the ideal physical body shapes and he wanted to be just like them. The trainer who had worked with hundreds of people immediately understood what the problem behind Steve's recent lackluster performance was. While Steve had the passion and the drive to work hard, he was suffering from insecurity. The trainer asked Steve to take down all the posters from his room and put up something that actually inspired him. Steve reluctantly took down all posters and put up a picture of him that had been taken a year ago. He was amazed when he recognized the transformation of his own body!

Mental health is a state of well-being in which the individual realizes his or her own abilities; can cope with the normal stresses of life; can work productively and fruitfully, and is able to make a contribution to his or her community. In the case of Steve, he was struck by doubt and discouragement. Once we allow these weak emotions to guide our actions, we become incompatible with our wellbeing. Like the importance of getting good exercise for our physical well-being, we need to think positively in order to exercise the brain for our mental wellbeing. Mental health includes the ability to enjoy life, to bounce back from adversity, and to achieve a balance. It also includes the ability to be flexible and adapt, the ability to feel safe and secure, and the ability to self-actualize. A wide range of factors contributes to and affects our mental state of health, and it is important to be aware of these factors. In that way, we can focus on the things we can control and work on those areas that need improvement.

Socioeconomic Status: Numerous studies across various scientific disciplines have shown that people with the least amount of education generally live in more difficult circumstances, which forces them to suffer the most sleep complaints, increased obesity rates, increased tendency towards criminal behavior, and higher risks of early death from heart disease.

Support: Family support stands at the foundation of how much we believe in our abilities and what we aspire to become. It is the ultimate drive that is blind to all barriers. A family supports us when we first come into the world. It nurtures us and gives us the tools and skills to go out into the world. Close and cordial families, therefore, have the greatest potential for raising individuals who hold the greatest promise and potential. Other supportive figures include friends who can guide us in decision-making, and help us get through difficult times. Our support system helps clarify our vision.

Culture: All cultures enjoy their particular traditions and festivities;

culture influences what we may wear, say, or find humorous. Western-Europeans and Americans tend to emphasize the individualism, while East-Asian cultures emphasize on collectivism – an individual is always seen in the context of other people and their environmental perspective. A simple way to describe the difference about how culture shapes us can be seen in the writings of the French writer René Descartes with his words, "*I think therefore I am,*" which he used to prove that if one wonders whether or not they exist, they therefore must exist since they are capable of such internal thoughts. Eastern Confucian philosophy emphasizes that a person cannot fully exist alone, and that he or she only reaches the highest form of existence once they mentally split the divide between themselves, others, and the environment.

Take care of your body. It's the only place you have to live. | Jim Rohn

Mental and physical health is a tool that helps repair the damage in our lives. Without these tools we would be like a mechanic in a busy workshop who has lots of work, but no tools to work with. Mark Twain said, "*The only way to keep your health is to eat what you don't want, drink what you don't like, and do what you'd rather not.*" Buddha sums up this idea with, "*The secret of health for both mind and body is not to mourn for the past, worry about the future, or anticipate troubles but to live in the present moment wisely and earnestly.*"

A healthy body and mind makes acceptance of, and reaction to **change** much more attainable...

15

Change

It is not the strongest of the species that survives, nor the most intelligent that survives. It is the one that is the most adaptable to change. | Charles Darwin

In today's progressive society change is constant and inevitable. Many of us think about the healthy changes we'd like to make in our lives to improve our circumstances, but unfortunately for many it does not work out. A principle that many people do not fully comprehend is that the least effective strategies are those that come from a place of fear or regret.

Enlightened self-interest encourages efficiency by doing *more per hour* instead of trying to do more hours in a day.

Change, like success, is a process and not an event. We learn some of the most valuable lessons of life through trial and error. Embracing change means getting along with people who may not possess the same skills as us. All successful companies have one thing in common; they bring together people with unique and differing skill-sets. While many can earn the money and not know how to manage it, others can manage it and not know how to earn it. We live in a society in which we cannot believe only in what we understand, neither is it a good time to doubt the ability of others. Times are changing so rapidly that what we once believed to be impossible is now possible.

Mother Nature no longer scares us with lightning, because what we once knew as a destructive supernatural force, we now harness as electricity. The age of cellular phone came to the grand stage in 1990's, and has changed the way we interact and do business. Rather than waiting for telegrams, we have embraced this fast-paced tool of interaction to become more efficient in our everyday lives. Every day we make new inventions, none of which would be possible without embracing change. In the words of George Santayana, "In a moving world readaptation is the price of longevity."

The principle of readaptation is what Dan M. discovered, just in time:

In 1970, Dan was the head of a successful meat packing family business located in the meatpacking district of downtown New York City. As Dan explains, "Our profits were significant, and our financial statements were healthy. We were growing at a rate of about 35% annually with sales that were strong in our home state of New York and steadily rising in Connecticut, New Jersey, and Rhode Island. Our quality was unmatched. We were respected in the community and I was earning a significant amount."

"Despite the fact that we were making strides in our business, I had an unsettling feeling that just would not go away. I was often worried about competition. We were a small company competing with national syndicates who could out promote, out-advertise, and underprice us at any time. In addition to our big national competitors, we had a host of regional producers small enough to provide superior service to customers who were virtually their neighbors. We were too big to have the small-town advantage and too small to have advantages of national scale. Our business was more vulnerable than it seemed."

What worried Dan more than the competition was the gap between potential and performance. The employees demonstrated lack of motivation, which resulted in lackluster performance. "Often I came to work and found our employees bored, seeing their mundane attitude and thoughtless mistakes. They frequently mislabeled products or failed to add the proper amount of seasoning to the precooked meals. While some drove the prongs of a forklift right through the packaged material, others would ruin a big batch of fresh meat by spraying it down with water while cleaning up the meat packing area. These were nuisances that were often costly even though no one was deliberately trying to waste money, time, or the material; it was just that no one took responsibility for their assigned task. I sure wasn't expecting anyone to commit to the company the way I was, but if we were going to survive the fierce competition, I needed to get everyone involved and on the same page. I needed to make everyone believe in the same goal and have a consistent vision."

Dan began searching for change. He knew he needed a solution to overcome the lackluster performance of all the employees. "I started by attending leadership seminars and reading books that would help me gain insight and understand how to get my employees to care about their jobs and the company that provided for their families. Not to anyone's surprise the search was not of much help. No one could explain to me how to motivate my own workforce; I was frustrated and had to figure things out on my own. However, deep down I always knew that I had started the company, so ultimately it was my duty to fix it. Rather than worrying about others, I needed to worry on my personal business strategy. It was my managerial style that kept people from taking responsibility. To my dismay the problem started with me, and fortunately I was the solution to the problem."

"I began asking myself what were the company's goals? How were we going to achieve these goals? Where did we want to be in the next 10 years? I had many questions, but no satisfying answers."

"I tried imagining what our company needed to do in order to withstand fierce competition and still have a solid market share.

My intuition was that I needed to rebuild an organization in which everyone had a say. Instead of having a system in which I was making all the decisions I needed to create an organization in which people took responsibility, ownership and pride in their work, in the product, and in the company. With this idea in mind, I knew that our product and quality of service would significantly improve, we would see growth and potential for expansion in the market."

"The idea of sharing responsibility first occurred to me while I was sitting in the park on a sunny Sunday afternoon watching Baxter, my golden retriever, playing with my 6-year-old daughter Tiffany. As I laid there watching the blue skies, I saw a flock of geese flying in a distinctive "V" formation, and like every other flock I had seen since I was a kid, I wondered why this was the case. This time I decided to unravel the mystery, little did I know that I was about to learn the most important lesson of my life from a flock of geese."

"The way animal experts explained this behavior was that when the flock flies together, the leading goose reduces air resistance for the goose behind it. This is to say each goose cuts the work in half for the goose behind. When a goose drops out of formation it quickly finds out that it requires a greater effort and energy to fly. That goose will quickly return to formation to take advantage of the lifting power that comes from flying together. Geese have mastered the genius idea of rotating leadership. The goose flying in the front expands most energy in an effort to provide an additional lift by decreasing air resistance for rest of the flock. In an effort to save energy the leading goose will drop out of the leading position to move to the rear where the air resistance is the lightest, while another goose takes the leading position. Consequently, the whole flock can fly 70% farther with the same amount of energy than an individual goose flying by itself."

"For years I had been trying so hard to make everyone follow my lead. In the process, I was wearing myself out without accomplishing anything. What I had failed to recognize all this time was that the old tyrannical methods of conducting my business were no longer acceptable. People have changed and so must I as a leader. Since the very first day I started this company, I viewed the financial aspect of business as the ultimate reward. The lackluster performance of the employees despite being well compensated, and their lack of commitment was no longer a mystery. I understood that money was not the ultimate drive for everyone. Since the employees had no stake in the company and no power to make decisions or control their own work, then why would they care much for the company?"

"The following morning I gathered the management team and announced that from now on everyone will have a say in how to maximize productivity of the company. The goal was to resolve any issues with solutions that came from the bottom up instead of the usual top to bottom approach of decision-making. I went from a strict authoritarian to a team player. At first, some of the employees were not happy with the idea because for them it meant increasing their responsibility, but I did not blame them. The fault was mine. For too long I had failed to share a vision that only I saw."

"Over the next two years the entire management system changed. Our company became a bigger success. As unsettling as giving up control had felt, deep down I knew it was the best decision for the future of the company. Starting from the management's newly detailed strategic and tactical plans that exceeded expectations; all the way to the delivery personnel delivering on time; the company was making major strides. All this took place while no one was laid off and no additional management team was recruited. Everything in the company remained the same; the only change was in approach, my perspective and me. In all my years of running the company as a successful owner, I had brought the company to *point A*, and had I not changed my strategic style of managing my company, I would only be able to bring us back to the same *point A*. Getting to *point B* meant I had to learn to be a coach of the team and not the principal player with the ball in his hands at all times."

In the words of George Bernard Shaw, "*When people shake their heads because we are living in a restless age, ask them how they would like to live in a stationary one, and do without change.*"

While change can be a challenging milestone in anyone's life, the key to change is behavior modification. If we can control the way we react to our circumstances, we can certainly shift the outcome to a more favorable one. To understand behavior change from a psychological perspective it is necessary to look at the five stages of trans-theoretical model, which comes from studies of alcohol, drug abuse, and smoking cessation. The other area where this model was previously applied is in health behaviors, including exercise and dieting. Clinicians and health educators use the trans-theoretical model to counsel patients, but no-one needs to be an expert to try this approach. Anyone motivated to change can use it to assess their situation and formulate strategies. While there is no specific rule about how we move from one stage to another, generally the order is as follows:

- Pre-contemplation
- Contemplation
- Preparation
- Action
- Maintenance

Pre-contemplation: This is the stage in which you are not intending to make a conscious change in the foreseeable future. Whether due to a lack of awareness or information or because you have failed in the past and feel demoralized. Often in this stage you put too much emphasis on the "cons" of changing your behavior. While you may be unaware that your behavior is problematic or produces negative consequences, the awareness and interest may be sparked by outside influences, such as public information campaigns, stories in the media, emotional experiences or family member's concern. To move past this stage we must think about the things we would most like to have in our lives; we must start to motivate ourselves.

Contemplation: At this stage you intend to change, and are often heard saying, "I will start in next 6 months." In reality, you often remain undecided for much longer than that. During this stage you are aware of the pros of changing but also can identify the cons. Ambivalence may lead you to weigh and re-weigh the benefits and costs: "If I stop smoking, I'll lose that hacking cough, but I know I'll gain weight," or "I know drinking could give me liver problems, but it helps me relax; if I quit, stress could kill me, too!"

The easiest way to unstick to these techniques is by listing the pros and the cons and then slowly picking away at them. For example, you may find it difficult to get regular exercise because it's inconvenient or you have too little time. If finding a 30-minute block of time to exercise is a barrier, how about planning two separate 15-minute sessions? Could someone else cook dinner so you can take a walk after work? If you feel too self-conscious to take an exercise class, how about buying an exercise video to use at home?

Preparation: This represents the stage where you have a plan and intend to take action in the immediate future – say, in a matter of weeks, if not days. For example, joining a health club, purchasing a supply of nicotine patches, or adding a calorie-counting book to the kitchen shelf. At this stage, it's important to anticipate potential obstacles. If you're preparing to cut down on smoking or alcohol, for example, be aware of situations that provoke these and avoid places that may tempt and plan ways around them. If work-stress triggers end-of-day drinking, plan to take a walk when you get home. If preparing dinner makes you want to smoke or drink, plan to have seltzer water instead of wine. If social situations are a problem, make a list of alternatives, such as going to the movies instead of having drinks or dinner with friends. This is the stage where individuals believe that changing their behavior can lead to a healthier life.

Simultaneously, it is important to build a realistic plan with achievable goals. If you've been sedentary and want to exercise more, start by making it your goal to avoid using the elevator for one, two, or three story trips. Or plan to walk 15 minutes every day. This can help you work your way up to more ambitious goals.

Action: This requires a combination of determination, dedication and devotion. This is the stage in which you make a behavioral change, say, you stop smoking, for example. This is when you need to practice the alternatives you identified during the preparation stage. For example, if stress tempts you to eat, you can use healthy coping strategies such as yoga, deep breathing, or exercise. At this stage, it's important to be clear about your motivation and if necessary, writing down your reasons for making the changes and reading them every day.

Maintenance: Once you have practiced the new behavior change for at least six months, this is the stage in which you would work to prevent relapse. This may be a challenge that requires other changes like avoiding situations or triggers associated with old habits. Even though this can be tough at times, it would mean to steer clear of certain activities and negative influences.

The late Steve Jobs once said, "*For the past 33 years, I have looked in the mirror every morning and asked myself: 'If today were the last day of my life, would I want to do what I am about to do today?' and whenever the answer has been 'No' for too many days in a row, I know I need to change something.*"

When we confront the possibilities of change, we must confront the borders or **limitations** that both define and guide us...

16

Limitations

The man with insight enough to admit his limitations comes nearest to perfection. | Goethe

Limitations are imaginary barriers that serve as hound dogs, tracking the scent of weakness to enslave our abilities and potential. Testing limits for some is a pleasurable hobby, while others live a life dwelling on their limitations. Live a life of the enthusiast and the sky is the limit. Live a life with imaginary limitations and decline is inevitable. The doing is not unfair; it is our own actions translating into consequences. Things just don't happen; they happen just. We create our own sorrow and our own happiness once we start to believe in the process of self-reliance. We pave our own ways knowing that others are limited in envisioning our potential. Yet so often, we behave in ways that fill the unconscious mind with doubts and insecurity, giving lame excuses for limitations. These are the beginnings of how limitations come about, and how they imprison our abilities and our vision for our life.

Every time we intentionally do less than our ability, we end up being less than we are; and treading this route a few years would be sufficient to render us incapable of keeping pace with changing times.

One look in the mirror and we can easily identify a foe from a friend. The problem lies within our own truth of existence. We become our own enemies when we decide to build barriers around our abilities, which is equivalent of signing a premature death warrant to our potential. Limitations are indeed shackles and only slaves wear shackles. We are no slaves. Whether we walk with a limp, or a broken neck, whether we are frail or whether circumstances hinder our journey, we still hold the key to our own freedom. We can choose to do what we say we can, or choose to avoid what we say we can't because it is a mental state that accepts or neglects its full potential.

For example, six months after joining his job as a news anchor, John B. was enjoying a fruitful career and many knew him as a hard-working man who knew no boundaries. He exceeded expectations when he landed a great job in a fraction of the time it took other news anchormen. John was well respected. At the pinnacle of his career he often thought that life just couldn't get any better. Back at his workplace John worked with a talented group of people. Some hard working than others, and some were smarter than others, but none more interesting than Nancy the typist.

For over a decade, Nancy had been working at the same desk, performing the same impeccable dictation of the featured headlines. As talented as Nancy was—as evidenced by the ten consecutive yearly awards that hung on her office wall—she always warmed to new tasks and greeted everyone enthusiastically.

One morning as John swung by Nancy's office to pick up a news story, he noticed she was not there. Another female typist handed the document to him. After flipping through the pages, John finally said to the woman, "There is something strange about Nancy."

"What do you mean?" asked the woman.

"Well, she is really good at what she does but her body language often seems unsynchronized with the environment around her."

The woman smiled and said, "John, you have been here for the last six months. Have you not noticed that Nancy is blind?"

In utter disbelief, he said, "That's just not possible. She greets everyone and types every report flawlessly. How could someone who is blind be a flawless typist and know who enters the room. And on top of that, win awards of excellence?"

The woman, smiling at John, said, "Well the first time anyone is introduced to her, she takes note of how to recognize them in the future by the sound of their footsteps. She has worked very hard at her professional skills and typing comes effortlessly to her."

John was blown away by Nancy's story and often used it as a reminder to himself that sometimes it takes true faith to overcome barriers. It is an art and a science to use the context of our life, instead of seeing limitations and surrendering to them.

We are all creators of our own destinies. In the future, we can work to not only meet but also exceed our expectations if we have an awareness and caution of the following roadblocks along the way:

- **Letting the past dictate the future**: Dwelling on what has happened in the past and allowing that to dictate your future is a recipe for disaster. If you need to recall the past in such detail, imagine it as a lesson learned in school instead of carrying it around like a backbreaking burden.

- **The unkind, wandering mind**: How significant is happiness? One of the ways in which scientists have attempted to answer this question is by sending surveys by email to a select group of people. These surveys were sent at different times of the day, and they simply asked the participants what they were doing a given time of the day, and if they were thinking about anything else while performing the task at hand. The final question was about how happy they were during these activities. What the survey revealed was that over 90% of the time people's minds wander as they perform their tasks. When wandering minds focused on a negative entity, people were ten times more likely to be unhappy then those who performed their tasks with their full attention. A similar situation occurs when people eat. When an individual eats a meal while thinking about the amount of work that remains undone, the meal is seldom enjoyed. Compare this to when a person eats when they are enjoying the company of fellow diners. Living in the present is healthy; living in the past is not. The best way to avoid this is by mentally being wherever we physically are.

- **Avoiding failure**: Failure is an essential step towards success. To enjoy future success, we must embrace failure and seek to learn from it whenever the opportunity presents itself. Failure is the process of trial and error. Our failed attempts can make us humble and destroy in sense of false pride. Always keep failure in perspective—failure is an event, not a person.

- **Changing others**: The ability to change the world lies not in others but within YOU. The idea is to generate happiness from deep within, rather than asking someone to do it for you. Additionally, when others find out that you are trying to change them, they may resent it. There will never be a right time to limit your happiness with regard to others. It is like going to someone else's birthday party hoping that we receive all the gifts.

- **Fix the broken**: Avoid complicating your life by trying to fix problems that are the results of isolated events. Focus instead on building lasting processes. If we get the processes right, the events that make up each process will fall into place. In other words, *don't be a dweller; be a propeller.*

In his poem titled "Turning Into Gods", Raul Rivera writes:

There is a revolution in the way that we think
Each day we push our bodies, thoughts, and voices to the brink.
Most of us most of the time, see the world through a very small
set of filters
We must break these filters and let our thoughts flourish instead
of die and wilter.
This is a time of communication, connection, and collaborative innovation
This will bring us progress and give humanly thought salvation
You use perhaps one millionth of the potential energy that's inside
your head
Lost in vibration, are the ideas that are said.
In my mind it is life that gives meaning to life and what we do with life
By preserving knowledge and science with the creation of music
and art are the gains of our strife.
In the science of today we become artist. In the art of today, we
become scientist
We use this to progress our species to become worldly finalist
There are no boundaries. There are no fears
We use this to accomplish and not look to our rears
Imagination allows us to think beyond our limitation-
It allows us to conceive of what might be -
And go farther that we ever thought possible
No idea ever to grand or radical
The point is in order to use your head you must go out of your mind
In order for you to gain the knowledge needed to unbind
You have to get beyond your routine ways of thinking
In order for your mind to be free of pollution and shrinking
We can break free of our genetic heritage
We have circled the moon, artificially reproduced DNA, and cut our
death percentage.
Why should death itself our last enemy be considered beyond
conquest?
We as humans have defined ourselves by overcoming biological
contests

We are teaching people how to use their head
And have their thoughts ultimately shed
You are ready to have your perspective about yourself and life
dramatically changed
And have your body thoughts and life go beyond the possible range
Because you will be a different person, and you should be ready to
face this possibility
Because soon we, ourselves will become whole new entities.

Until the time these are mastered, limitations must be identified and respected; as insulation against the perils of uncontrolled **anger**...

17

Anger

Holding on to anger is like grasping a hot coal with the intent of throwing it at someone else; you are the one who gets burned. | Buddha

Anger is most useful when it is channeled into something constructive. Anger is an emotion, a very basic one. Aristotle says, "Anybody can become angry - that is easy, but to be angry with the right person and to the right degree and at the right time and for the right purpose, and in the right way – that is not within everybody's power and is not easy." Anger is a natural, healthy human emotion that builds confidence in situations that may be threatening or present a danger to our loved ones. While rational anger can be constructive in allowing you to feel competent to confront dangerous situations, when this emotion is felt in abundance it can easily become destructive. This can lead to problems at work, in our personal relationships, and in the overall quality of our lives. Before you know it, you can feel as though you are at the mercy of an unpredictable and an overpowering emotion.

Excessive anger can numb us mentally and emotionally. Therefore, addressing these emotions along the way is extremely important.

A research study suggests that expressing anger in effective ways is a healthy behavior that can accomplish tasks and also prevent medical related issues. Researchers found that people who suppressed anger were found to have more anxiety and depression than the general population.[1] Often anger is the byproduct of perceived loss of control over factors that affect our integrity. In other cases, we become angry because of our inability to meet personal or social expectations. How fast this emotion turns into rage is dependent upon how much unexpressed anger and perceived failure finally flows to the surface. Despite having the understanding that expressing anger does not often lead to a positive change, it just might be the only instinct we've learned in coping with stressful situations. Such instinctive behavior can cost us everything from friendships and to important family relationships.

After a long day of work, Bill got a ride home with Sam, his colleague at the office. During the trip the two shared their stories about their busy day at the office. As Sam approached Bill's house, Bill insisted that he be dropped off a block ahead of his house, and when his colleague asked him why, Bill just kept silent. Getting a bit worried, Sam asked Bill if everything was fine. Bill, who was now staring out of the window at the gloomy clouds in the sky, replied that he and his wife were going through a divorce and that he had moved to a smaller studio apartment a block away from his family. "But that's not all," said Bill. "This is my third divorce and I just don't know what to do. Each time I get divorced it is because I have let anger build up inside of me for months, and each time I explode with rage. This behavior has cost me my inner peace. I can't help it. I am hopeless and lonely."

Unexpressed anger can lead to pathological expressions, such that we may feel the need to get back at people without telling them why, rather than confronting them constructively. Unexpressed anger can also make us seem cynical and hostile. If you find yourself speaking contemptuously, criticizing everything, and making cynical comments, you may have failed to learn the constructive expressions of angry emotions. Undoubtedly, this will have an affect on your relationships, both personal and professional.

While trying to suppress our anger by not speaking about it, we run the risk of converting an outward conflict into an inward issue. This kind of behavior can cause complications including but not limited to, high blood pressure, heart problems and depression. Therefore, it is important that we address anger by restructuring our thought process so that we can begin to deal with it in a healthy manner.

For example, when a person is angry, rather than keeping silent or using colorful language, it is better to say to yourself, "I know this is frustrating, and it's understandable that I'm upset, but this is not the end of the world and letting anger get the best of me will not fix this problem."

Using this logic we can defeat anger because even if our anger is justified, it can easily become irrational without giving us any notice. We can achieve a healthy perspective through autosuggestion by using statements like, "It's not the end of the world, just relax," or "This too shall pass" or "With this in the past, better times are ahead."

Here is one of my favorite parables about anger:

A senior monk and a junior monk were traveling together. At one point, they came to a river with a strong current. As the monks were preparing to cross the river, they saw a very young and beautiful woman also attempting to cross. The young woman asked if they could help her. The senior monk carried this woman on his shoulder, forded the river and let her down on the other bank. The junior monk was very upset, but said nothing. As they walked away, the senior monk noticed that his junior was suddenly silent and enquired, "Is something the matter, you seem very upset?" The junior monk replied, "As monks, we are not permitted to touch a woman. How could you then carry that woman on your shoulders?" The senior monk replied, "I left the woman on the bank a long time ago however, you seem to be carrying her still."

In this story, we see how the older monk with his mind free was able to see a situation, respond to it, and continue to be present on the journey. The younger monk, however, was bound by ideas, held on to them for hours, and, in doing so, missed the experiences of the next part of the journey.

Mental attachment to an idea or earlier experience blocks the full experience of the present here and now. Attachments slow the mind, interfering with appropriate responses to the immediate situation.

Here are five simple steps to monitor anger. With practice these steps become ever-more effective.

- **Be Aware**: Familiarize yourself with the triggers that set you off. Is it someone at your job? Someone you know at the local store? Whoever it is and whatever it is, if we recognize the triggers, we can control the way we react to our circumstance.

- **Who does it best**: Find yourself a role model who handles adversity without losing their cool. Once this happens, you can then use them as your template to understand how to deal with adversity.

- **Warning signs**: Pay attention to your body language. As the alarms begin to go off, alerting you to the danger that your anger is building. Pay attention to your gut feeling, to a nose twitch or teeth grinding and changes in breathing patterns. These may be the signs that tell you that you are getting angry.

- **Take a break**: When anger is running rampant, just count to ten or take a time out. You can ask yourself if what you are upset about is worth being upset about.

- **Let's do it again**: It is OK to stumble, slip and fall. The important message here is to use the lessons learned at any future opportunity.

In the words of Ambrose Bierce, "*Speak when you are angry and you will make the best speech you will ever regret.*"

Anger is but an emotion, and can be channeled or neutralized, clearing the part for true achievement, **the art of doing...**

18

The Art of Doing

If you can't get a miracle, become one | Unknown

A priest who had spent his entire life preaching once took a cab. At the end of the journey the preacher scolded the driver and told him that through the entire journey the preacher said prayers and feared for his life. The preacher also pronounced that the driver would go to hell, as he not only endangered his own life but the life of the passenger and everyone on the road due to reckless driving. A few years later the preacher died and was ushered into heaven and given two wings as a reward for his services to God. The preacher during his tour of heaven came across someone familiar and enquired who this person was; to his dismay it was the cab driver and had six wings and a flute. The preacher went to the angels and said, "I am not complaining, but how do you explain this situation: a preacher gets two wings and a reckless driver gets six wings and a flute?" The angel replied in heaven rewards are results-oriented. You preached and every one fell asleep. He drove and put the fear of God in everyone he came across."

Whatever we do, we will be more successful if we do it with honesty, fairness and to the best of our ability. Too often we say one thing and do another. This cat-and-mouse game leads us far away from the true purpose of life. We must act as we think, even though thinking is easy and acting is quite the contrary. The more we delay, the greater the danger of disappointment. While actions themselves can result in disappointment, the chances of failing are reduced. Sitting idle increases these chances with great certainty. We seldom fail when we aim high and miss; we fail when we aim low and hit.

A pilot friend of mine once spoke about the four forces of flying: Lift, Drag, Thrust and Weight. These four forces also exist within us. We can choose to be the lifters and the thrusters or we can merely weigh down and drag our lives at a turtle's pace. Life is too short to travel at a turtle's pace if we aspire to achieve our dreams! These dreams get compromised because of an overbearing lack of will. Family, friends and mentors with positive, practical attitudes can lift and thrust.

For as long as the human race has existed, uncertainty has been a central dilemma. To move past this point we must recognize that remaining idle breeds uncertainty, and the art of doing is the one pure act that nurtures certainty. Starting something new is the way of becoming a doer, because at the end of the day, hearing the words "well done" will always outdo the words "well said."

Nature has its own glorious ways of demonstrating the forces that generate and sustain life. What is to become of the living creatures of this world if these forces cease to exist? Will there be life? Similarly, what of the personal internal force that generates progress? If this force comes to a halt, what is to become of our progress? Will the mind grow and expand its thinking abilities without it? Or will it decay and simply atrophy? A person in action is a person progressing. Without this movement, the race stays unfinished. In the same way that the cold of winter forces us to put on our coats and button up for the safety of our health, life requires that we must use the act of doing to generate results for our own good. When you button your coat and miss the first buttonhole it is not the end of the world. You simply start again. We do not succeed in achieving our dreams without the first act of doing, whether it is successful or not.

When was the last time we heard that a *critic* fought valiantly on a battlefield, in the midst of an actual war, and then later went on to win an honorable reward? Critics usually hide behind a pen, a keyboard or a microphone. They seldom face true adversity with its inherent risks. It is seldom *critics* who win acclaim from action; it is the soldiers, and the people who are in action, who move and struggle and persevere. It is these "doers" who deserve such recognition. We cannot possibly think about moving the world with our thoughts alone, without actually moving ourselves as well. In the words of Mark Twain, "Action speaks louder than words but not nearly as often." It is better to do, fail and profit by the wisdom born out of failure than to sit down in unexpressed genius and atrophy from disuse.

In a world where we can no longer plan or predict our way to success, how can we achieve our goals and dreams? It's a question that puzzles the very best of us. However, in today's society, just like any other historical society where change was the only constant, it is a question we must answer. This is true whether we are innovators or entrepreneurs, managers or brand new graduates. The first and most important step is to, "Just start." To further simplify this, it is better to take action now and learn on the fly. This approach can serve as a forecasting tool by which we can shrug off that nagging frustration that comes with constant uncertainty. Action distills for us the very essence of what makes people successful in today's volatile society.

In this day and age your brain is flooded with knowledge through mass media and other resources of instant information. Having this knowledge is not good enough; we must strive to apply it. Willing is not good enough; we must act. Never worry about how big the task is and whether or not you can finish. Just learn to start because only God alone can finish. God only helps those who help themselves.

Being self-aware is the work of a wise man that understands the urgency of time and the need for action. As Baltasar Gracian explains, "*The wise man does at once what a fool does finally.*" Sir Henry Wadsworth Longfellow talks about the importance of time and action when he said, "*It takes less time to do a thing right, than it does to explain why you did it wrong.*"

Getting things done makes you look good; it helps your **appearance.** It builds up an impression in the minds and hearts of those you meet...

19

Appearance

Appearance rules the world | Friedrich Schiller

Never in the history of the human race has appearance played a more important role in shaping our society. In these modern times, the way in which we communicate has outgrown the basic communicative needs of our ancestors. From Skype to phones to emails and from mass media to social media, we communicate in ways that makes ideas available instantly. However, the hunger for communication only grows from a technological perspective to a more personal phase that becomes a decisive step in determining whether or not we attract success. This personal stage is none other than our appearance.

Consider the symbolic hair of Donald Trump, Conan O'Brien or Hulk Hogan and the peculiar look and speaking style of Arnold Schwarzenegger and Sylvester Stallone. These are some of the most successful people in their respective industries, and they understand how to make every appearance count. If we do not take pride in our personal appearance, than we run the risk of selling ourselves short. What are the chances of going to a job interview and landing that job if you look like you just woke up? A college survey that interviewed 150 employers reported the number one reason for rejecting someone after the interview was poor appearance. When you do not take pride in your appearance the hiring party may perceive this as a lack of respect either for yourself or towards the company.

This principal of appearance applies not just in the professional field but also in the personal field. An elegant dresser has greater self-confidence and courage. Our appearance is a sensory impression that reaches those we interact with, primarily through the sense of sight. This is often the time people are forming a lasting opinion about who we are. Those who understand this powerful message make the best use of it. We can influence the way people perceive us during initial contact simply by the way we dress.

Scientific research explains how physical environment can impact our mental environment. Researchers explain that to a certain degree, we create our physical environment by the way we dress. In today's society books are judged by their cover; houses are appraised by the community they are located in, and people are judged by their behavior and their physical appeal. In the perfect world this is neither ethical nor moral, but the facts remain. Many of us believe what lies on the inside far outweighs external appearance and while this may be true, what is on the inside does not come out instantly. A person's inner goodness is not readily apparent and as a result opportunities can be lost.

While we cannot control every aspect of our appearance, we can control the way we present ourselves. Transformational learning teaches us to bring about change in the most noticeable areas. This transformation can certainly start from the way we look at our wardrobe to the eloquence of our speech. Personal grooming and eliminating bad language are two quick ways to develop a well-sought confidence that paves the way for success. Appropriate dressing is not a luxury; it is a necessity for those striving for the very best. Personal appearance is a form of nonverbal communication that demonstrates our competence, elegance, knowledge and confidence. We must keep in mind that at the end of the day, it is honey, not vinegar that attracts.

Various studies indicate how 7% of our interaction with someone is based on the words we use; 38% of the interaction comes from the tone of our voice, and the final 55% comes from a combination of our appearance and our body language. Successful business people take advantage of this fact on a daily basis by making a good impression when meeting new clients and maintaining a successful body language with old clients, colleagues and employees.

Even when no one else is watching, we can still see ourselves up to fifty-five times a day in elevators, mirrors, computer screens, phones and windows. These are fifty-five opportunities to generate a positive feeling and to ensure a correct image!

Social psychologists explain that most of us form the first impression of others in the first thirty seconds. The history of these ingrained instincts can be dated thousands of years back when survival depended on instincts. Only the fittest survived. Oscar Wilde writes, "*It is only shallow people who do not judge by appearances. The true mystery of the world is visible, not the invisible.*"

Besides personal appearance there is another kind of appearance that affects the way we behave or feel. Think about working in a disorganized environment, with dirty floors and chaos all around. These environments are stressful and can translate negatively into your personal life. Such an environment lowers enthusiasm and work productivity. Now take into consideration a clean, organized working environment. This will always produce lasting positive effects. Employers now more than ever are paying close attention to the finer details that boost performance in spite of the cost. From heating and lighting, open vs. closed space, flexibility, sustainability and the ergonomic designs and latest technology, employers understand that top businesses reflect personality and culture. On average we spend 40 hours a week at our workplace, and therefore making the work environment serene and inspiring is always favored for successful businesses.

Going to a funeral well dressed and groomed is a sign of paying respect to the deceased and to the grieving family. While clothes and manners don't make the man, they surely improve his appearance. To feel like a million dollars, we must learn to present ourselves as such through our mannerism and appearance.

There was once a stubborn king with a missing eye and a leg. He called for all the painters of his kingdom and asked them to paint a beautiful portrait of him. Everyone tried, none succeeded, and as a result they were all imprisoned. Eventually one painter made a portrait to the king's liking and was handsomely rewarded. The lesson here is that not everyone can see our inner beauty. Therefore they will judge us on our appearance. Instead of being resentful, it is our responsibility to make sure we present ourselves like a gem so that others perceive us as such. In the words of George Bernard Shaw, "*Better keep yourself clean and bright; you are the window through which you see the world.*"

When you look good, and when you feel good, good things come to you. You find yourself on the **winner's** track...

20

Win, Win, Win

The will to win, the desire to succeed, the urge to reach your full potential... these are the keys that will unlock the door to personal excellence. | Confucius

The idea of winning is a powerful motor that drives many so-called winners. For those people, winning isn't everything; it's the only thing. It is a way of life. These winners are battle-tested veterans that understand the importance of winning before actually winning.

Unlike the rest, winners understand that we choose our victories or losses long before we experience them. Winners know that mindset is an all-powerful entity and that it can conquer anything if it is fixated on the goal. Winners take it upon themselves to create an atmosphere of excitement, enthusiasm and high intellectual and moral purpose. They work hard to develop and maintain a combination of intelligences: the logical capacity to figure out options; the linguistic capacity to persuade and motivate others and the interpersonal knowledge to appreciate human potential. They think of themselves in high regard, because they believe that the only way to share good things with others is to first obtain it for themselves. Rather than worrying, they stay positive and expect good things to occur. This attitude helps lift the spirits of everyone around them.

These focused, optimistic people utter the right words in any given situation to saturate the minds around them with enough positive weaponry to ward off any negative thinking. Nobody is perfect, of course, and nobody can be expected to say the right thing all the time. Winners however, accept their mistakes and they move on. They put it down to experience. Winners understand that if the present is spent dwelling on the past, then the future will remain uncertain, and uncertainty does not exist in a winner's vocabulary. *Winners make things happen, while losers let things happen.*

Psychologists who have studied the most successful people in any society explain that the one thing winners have in common is a positive self-image. Winners control their circumstances through their obsession with positivity. There are other people in the race also. There are those who try, but fail. These people are not losers. They are winners who have not yet won; they share the same positive mental attitude, self-image, dedication and focus. All the winners of the world have failed many times on their way up. None of these people are losers, they are winners in their own minds first, and it is only a matter of time before they become winners "out in the open" for everyone to see.

On the other hand, there are those who are accustomed to losing and actually prefer to stay in the negative emotional depths. These are the individuals who discourage others in order to feel personal superiority with minimum effort. These are the individuals that want to do the least to gain maximum reward even if that means taking credit for other peoples' work. These people are intolerant and contemptuous of others. They encourage misery in themselves and then they spread it to others.

Winners on the other hand are enthusiastic individuals who work more than they are being paid for, believing that it is an investment in their own future. They are the positive motivators that encourage some and challenge others to invoke the alchemy of great potential. Winners are tolerant and are seen as extraordinary confidence boosters through their understanding of how to project positive self-image into exemplary leadership. These leaders understand that any act of winning requires self-discipline.

Discipline is the bridge between goals and accomplishments. Self-discipline is an important principle that determines the worth of a person. It is a principle that separates those who can talk the talk from those who can walk the walk. The word self-discipline may cause resistance and discomfort, depending on how you perceive it; some may perceive it as punitive and authoritarian. On the other hand, some may see self-discipline as a personal trainer that teaches the work ethic necessary to achieve, in accordance to each individual's aspirations.

There are those who believe that our lives are predestined, and that our horoscopes cannot be altered. Self-discipline on the other hand has no set criteria, it is free expression of inner strength that teaches us that we are in charge of our own destinies, and that one can achieve any goal or desire if the will to make small sacrifices is present. Being self-disciplined means being a visionary and seeing the greater picture, while others indulge themselves in smaller gratifications. We are often our own biggest obstacles, and self-discipline is the slow moving bulldozer that flattens the surface for a smoother ride. This principle teaches us patience, persistence, perseverance, self-control and most importantly, it teaches self-reliance.

To understand the psychology of winning we must pay close attention to the words we choose to communicate our thoughts and beliefs. Much of our day is spent interpreting our surroundings. It is as if we are developing an inner voice, which gives expression to conscious and unconscious thoughts. While some of this inner voice may be productive, eighty percent of the time it leads to unrealistic, self-defeating and negative self-talk, which is the number one cause of depression.

We can alter our moods and attitude by using positive self-talk to achieve the mindset we wish to achieve. For example, when stuck in a heavy traffic jam, a person with a losing attitude may become contemptuous of his environment and say, "Why do I have to be stuck in this traffic? Why are people so incompetent in driving? I should not have taken this route. This is just unbearable." These thoughts only raise your anxiety and anger. If you have a winning attitude and use a more optimistic view, you will see better alternatives to deal with the current circumstances. You might choose to say, "This should give me enough time to listen to at least one chapter in my audio book," or "This should buy me some time to clear my mind of any previous negative thoughts that I feel are important to address." This attitude generates a calm sense of peace and tranquility, which in turn makes winners feel in control of their circumstances.

Positive self-talk generates satisfaction and happiness through the release of a morphine-like substance called endorphins. Endorphins are the body's natural euphoric drugs and they alleviate pain, reduce anxiety, enhance the immune system and slow the aging process.

A winner knows that in the game of life, winning is not an isolated event. There are no breaks, compromises or excuses. If you wish to achieve a goal then you must start by establishing good habits. People who enjoy misery expect sickness, failure and disappointments. People with a winning attitude expect health, prosperity and happiness.

Optimism is better than pessimism; faith is better than doubt. Optimism can help you restore faith in yourself, whereas pessimism can misguide even the righteous. Good things tend to flow towards the person who already appears to have abundance.

Winners have a clear vision of their destination, because winners understand that without a clear destination, a long car ride may end up nowhere. Aiming at nothing only ensures that we will hit it every time. Winners understand that money does not grow on trees and therefore they thrive on being proactive. The approach must be to focus on the important things in life and put off the least important things for later. Watching television or online chatting can wait if something more important requires our attention. Prioritizing is the key to success.

The most important characteristic of a winner is persistence. While we all have ups and downs in life, a winner never budges. He or she is able to perform at a peak level even under pressure. Winners do not fear rejection. To a winner, rejection is a temporary setback that can be changed through persistence. In fact, winners see failures and rejections as a good source of feedback. Here are opportunities that can improve knowledge and elevate skills. Winners have a purpose behind each action, whereas losers lose faith half way because they lack reasoning.

Having positive, goal-oriented people around you as a support group is an important step towards establishing a winning life. A support group of just two to four members is enough. This is your steering committee, your advisory board. Availing yourself of this kind of support helps a winning-minded individual state loudly, "I take my success very seriously."

Life's winners tend to abstain from criticizing, complaining, or being complacent. They don't have time for that. For them the reward lies in being, becoming and always remaining part of the solution. They show appreciation for kindness, and forgiveness for cruelty. Winners show enthusiasm, from the way they greet people, to the positive way they respond to a simple "How are you?" Their winning habit blooms many times throughout the day. As Ralph Waldo Emerson writes, "*That which we persist in doing becomes easier, not that the nature of the thing has changed, but our ability to do has increased.*"

There needs to be balance in all things, and with the desire to win comes the need for awareness of others and the ability to **understand the feelings of others**...

21

Empathy

The great gift of human beings is that we have the power of empathy. |
Meryl Streep

Empathy is a divine emotion that is cultivated in the human heart and spirit. Wrapped inside empathy are the traits of tolerance, forgiveness, and the ability to understand others. Empathy is the emotion that allows us first to perceive and then adapt other people's perspectives. It is a spontaneous and a natural process that helps us to tune into the pain and needs of others without any personal bias. However, to understand why empathy is the essence of a complete human being, it is first necessary to focus on our human moral intelligence.

Just as cognitive intelligence helped the human species develop a theoretical and a practical understanding of the world, moral intelligence helps us expand our understanding of the principles of right or wrong and good or evil. Our moral intelligence teaches us that a good will is intrinsically good; its value is wholly self-contained and utterly independent of its external relations. Actions are morally right in virtue of their motives, which must derive more from duty than from inclination. Moral intelligence does not rely on incentives in this world or the one hereafter. Our children demonstrate the fact that moral actions do not focus on self-interest; rather they are focused on the best interest of others. For example, when a child cries, another child often tries to console the crying child by offering toys or comfort. Toddlers bury their faces in their mothers' lap or call for the attention of an adult. These are all examples that demonstrate how children who know nothing of incentives can feel empathy which indeed cultivates their moral intelligence.

A convicted killer on death row was interviewed about the heinous killing of five teenage girls whom he first raped and then later choked to death at different intervals. The killer's response was devoid of empathy. He felt that the provocative clothing that the girls wore was an open invitation. He said, "It was the welcome mat laid out in front of his neighbor's house." The killer's lack of morality, based on how he rationalized his actions, bears witness that without empathy there would only be chaos.

In another instance, a man backing his car into a parking spot backed in too fast and damaged the front bumper of the rear car, which was unattended. There were no witnesses at the site of the crash. This man was educated, employed and late for work. After hearing the thud he got out of his car and wrote a brief note on the back of his business card and left it under the windshield wiper. Considering that his car did not receive any damage, the offender could have easily left without leaving his business card. But he decided to take responsibility and morally do the right thing. This is a case where empathy generates morality.

We are able to empathize with the ones we love much easier than strangers or even those we barely know. Take for example the situation between two acquaintances: while shopping for school supplies for her children, Susan ran into Kelly (the parent of a child who shared a class with Susan's child) in the stationery aisle. Out of common courtesy Susan asked, "How are you?" Kelly replied, "Not so well, my mother passed away yesterday." After chatting for a few minutes Susan said, "Please let me know if there is anything I can do for you," and off she went. Within moments, she was nowhere in sight while Kelly remained in the store feeling lonely and bereft at the loss of her mother.

Too often we offer hollow words of concern to others without these words holding any actual meaning. We offer superficial, non-genuine and sometimes ritualistic empathy. Our self-centered approach to life has us worried about our own problems first and therefore we might see Kelly's concern as a disturbing emotion that disrupts the equilibrium of our own mental peace. However, genuine empathy would influence our morally aware selves to share Kelly's concern in the same way we would share concern for someone close to us. Even when we have not experienced the exact same type of grief or trauma – for example in Susan's case, if her own mother had not passed away – she might not be sure how to "feel" or know how to be of help. However the idea of empathizing with someone is to understand the emotion of losing a loved one. Can you correlate the emotions of losing someone you love with the way it would make you feel? Would you appreciate someone regularly checking up on you to see if you are OK? These are the questions we must ask ourselves in order to understand genuine empathy.

Understanding why people behave the way they do, and why they act the way they do is almost a lost art.. First, we must learn to stop passing judgments. Too often we call someone unethical or immoral based on the way they've behaved or the way they've chosen to act. However, when we picture ourselves in their shoes, we can easily justify those actions and rationalize those behaviors. Once we understand that it is not just the person, but also the circumstances and the environment that dictates behavior, we have a clearer picture. We must become compassionate and empathetic towards others to live in a world of harmony. In the New Testament (Luke 10:29-37), the story of the Good Samaritan reads:

*"A man was travelling from Jerusalem to Jericho, and he fell
among robbers, who stripped him and beat him and departed,
leaving him half dead. Now by chance a priest was going down
the road; and when he saw him he passed by on the other side.
So likewise a Levite, when he came to the place and saw him,
he passed by on the other side. But a Samaritan, as he jour-
neyed, came to where he was; and when he saw him, he had
compassion, and went to him and bound his wounds, pouring on
oil and wine; then he set him on his own beast and brought him
to an inn, and took care of him. And the next day he took out
two dinars and gave them to the innkeeper, saying, 'Take care
of him; and whatever more you spend, I will repay you when I
come back.' Which of these three, do you think, proved neighbor to him who fell among the robbers? He said, 'The one who
showed mercy on him.' And Jesus said, 'Go and do likewise.'*

Empathy is a principle of morality that will guide us to do the right
thing in every circumstance. When we become emotionally unsen-
timental we forget to be honorable. We have a tendency to become
insensitive and hurtful. It is through empathy, the divine emotion
of the human heart that we learn to become caring. It is through
empathy that we cultivate a moral intelligence. D.D. Meyers, while
analyzing presidential thoughts and actions, said, "*While eschewing
emotion – and its companion, vulnerability – Obama should be careful
not to sacrifice empathy, the 'I feel your pain' connection that sustained
Clinton. This connection is the shorthand people use to measure their
leaders' intentions. If people believe you're on their side, they will trust
your decisions.*"

As empathy grows, so does the solidity of your character and your
word...

22

My Word, My Bond

Honesty is conforming our words to reality; integrity is conforming reality to our words. | Stephen Covey

Golfing legend Jack Nicklaus was grief-stricken over the death of a grandchild and he refused to take part in the biggest golf tournament of the year. Yet when asked about two smaller tournaments that he was already scheduled to compete in, he said he would play as he had already made the promise.

At one stage or another we have all made promises; some are kept and some are broken. But have we ever given much thought to whether we fulfill a promise or not? Back when our word was our covenant, we thought long and hard before making a promise, as our word meant so much to our character and how society would perceive us. When our word was stronger than any contract a court system could impose, we prospered as a society.

However, we have traveled far from those ancestral roots. In to-day's society the common phrase "Get it in writing" creates trust anarchy. Whether it's the ease of not making the effort to fulfill a promise or the displeasure from the hardship of fulfilling a promise, for one reason or another, we have committed ourselves to cynicism. This in turn, makes our society a dangerous place. Nowadays there are no moral ramifications for breaking a promise. We have become less resistant to making promises even if we have no intentions of keeping them.

Dr. Michael (Mike) Macari was a collaborator on a scientific research project that involved a number of other researchers. The project lasted a few months and around deadline time it was clear that everyone was running late. When Mike was contacted to check the status of his part of the project, he promised he would deliver the project on time. And he did. Two weeks after completing the project, a colleague tried contacting Mike various times via email in order to obtain his signature on a "conflict of interest" form so that the final manuscript could be submitted to the intended journal. It was only after calling Mike's office, did anyone discover that Mike had been battling gastric cancer for 16-months and as a result had passed away. In fact, just weeks before he died, Mike had been told that his cancer was malignant and as a result he was bed-ridden. Even while immersed in pain and tragedy, Mike kept his word and fulfilled his promise to complete the project. He lived with integrity and values that remain an inspiration to all who knew Mike.

In our busy, high-speed world, we often do not realize or accept that some of our strained relationships are the outcome of a broken or empty promise. The unpredictability of life can often put us in situations where we might not be able to keep our promises. But even that is understandable to others if it is explained and not repeated. However, a definite pattern in breaking promises sends out a negative message; one that can make people feel disrespected or unappreciated, as with the story of Stacey and Kyle:

Stacey and Kyle had been enjoying the "early stages" of dating. They had been out just twice. After going out on a third date, Kyle promised Stacey that he would call her the following day after work. Stacey eagerly awaited Kyle's call since the two were just getting to know each other and particularly because Stacey was interested in keeping in contact. However, the following day just before Kyle was about to call Stacey, he received a business call and consequently forgot about calling Stacey. He later texted her to apologize and promised that he would call the next day. The following day, Kyle was busy calling his clients and forgot about her again. This time Stacey sent a text to remind Kyle that it was the second time he had not called. He said he forgot, apologized, and once again promised. Unfortunately, he did not keep this promise either. This last broken promise was the final straw for Stacey. She decided he was not worth the wait. Kyle never made the effort to call again because he felt too guilty.

Fulfilling a promise is an indirect way of communicating appreciation, value and empathy. A broken promise can lead to resentment, anxiety, missed opportunities, lack of trust, and feelings of inadequacy. Unfulfilled promises arouse a feeling of false competence; they keep us in a state of regret and arrest any personal growth or opportunity for success. A key attribute of success is that we place value in others and keep our promises to demonstrate integrity. We cannot function as a society without the institution of promises and the assurance of their fulfillment. We make agreements and covenants, which help create families and clans. These covenants are the basis of our collective lives, which help us build well-organized units. You may find that if you do not abide by your promises, you may suffer from a feeling of uncertainty and unrest. You may even find yourself in a state of perpetual conflict. Therefore it is only fitting that we resist making empty promises, and strive to fulfill those we have already made. We should also remind ourselves that if we cannot keep our promise, than we should not make one.

In order to get in the habit of keeping promises and abiding by covenants, it is important that we start the training process very early in childhood. This is because a child emulates the actions and words of the parents, and therefore, parents have the opportunity to be role models in their actions. Naturally children expect that promises will be kept, but when these promises are taken lightly, children take the negative example and develop a habit of not keeping their own word. The psychological explanation behind this phenomenon is that children learn to rationalize their behavior through constant observation, and they will often say, "If he/she does not keep their promise, than why should I?" We all dearly love our children. We treat them with fairness and kindness. We teach them various principles of life in the hopes of seeing them succeed in the future. While we expect them to learn and be their best, it is our responsibility that when we make a promise we must fulfill it without fail. It is the way of living an honest life; a life that rejuvenates the soul and solidifies our belief in those that surround us.

The other form of a promise that we often make is the one that we make to ourselves. Whether that promise is to lose weight, work hard, quit smoking, spend more time with family, do well in school, or for the betterment of any other aspect of our lives, we must strive to fulfill these promises to uplift our inner spirits and raise the standards of self-expectation. Self-promises serve our interest in having effective authority over ourselves. This sense of authority empowers us to become the captains of our own ships, and therefore we can pick and choose our own destination.

Every New Year's Day millions of us make self-promises. By March, 80% will have already broken those promises. The problem does not lie in the obstacles set in our paths, but rather in our will to persevere through these obstacles. Oftentimes our feet become rooted among the obstacles we set out to cross. Therefore, we must allow self-promises to serve as the greater force that when applied, can break all the chains of unhealthy habits. Understanding then, that self-promises affect our self-esteem, confidence, and experience of life, here are five tips that can help any one of us regain control of our lives and become more productive members of our society:

1. **Knowledge is power**. What we don't know will hurt us and ignorance therefore is not bliss. It is important to know and to be certain that whichever commitment you make, you can follow. To fulfill a promise, it is necessary to be clear about the expectation, action, and the expected outcome. Next, set a deadline. This will help the unconscious mind to facilitate a strategy that can be used to execute any task.

2. **Writing is essential**. Never hold things to a faulty memory as it can begin to fade without any warning. If you have made a promise, write it down. Delivering on time can be the difference between success and failure. Save yourself the embarrassment by not forgoing the process of writing.

3. **Make it count**. Make the smaller promises and avoid the big ones you might not fulfill. This is an excellent way of building a trustworthy reputation. A true measure of a person is not by the size of the promises made, but by the conviction in seeing the promise through to the end.

4. **Act**. Do not make excuses or master the art of rationalization. If you have committed yourself to a difficult promise, then ask more of yourself. Persist, push yourself and work a little longer, no matter the cost. Success is the result of high quality of relationships. Therefore, learning to hold promises as sacred agreements without any room for excuses is the fast track to achieving goals and dreams.

5. **We reap what we sow**. Expect the best of people, if you have delivered as you said you would. Learn to trust others until they prove otherwise. Give people the chance to prove themselves. This approach allows you to surround yourself with more dependable people. Surrounded by those you trust will allow you to reach the goal of peace of mind.

Keeping our promises strengthens our commitments in both our personal and professional lives. More importantly, it highlights our moral character. By organizing our promises and breaking them down into smaller tasks, we empower our will to do. Unlike politics where there is typically a major massacre of promises, religion holds a promisor accountable for the greater good of mankind. In his book *The Reader*, Bernhard Schlink writes, "*Is this what sadness is all about? Is it what comes over us when beautiful memories shatter in hindsight because the remembered happiness fed not just on actual circumstances but on a promise that was not kept?*" Similarly in her book *Distant Shores*, Kristin Hannah writes, "*Promises were a lot like impressions. The second one didn't count for much.*"

Integrity builds a capacity for **visualization** of future greatness...

23

Visualizing the Future

It is not in the stars to hold our destiny but in ourselves | *William Shakespeare*

It is important to remember that we cannot become what we intend to be by remaining what we are. Being able to plan out the future allows us to seek after opportunities. Having an understanding and more importantly, a strategy of how we want our future to turnout in the next five years or ten years, serves as our game plan to win the game of life. In the world of sports, no team goes out on the playing field without having a strategy in place. Champions often tell tales of how they first visualized the whole process before they actually executed the plan to win.

As mentioned earlier, failing to plan is the same as planning to fail. However if we put our mind to a task, we can overcome any obstacle. We must understand that we hold power over our problems and not the other way around. We must visualize the process of winning every day, until it becomes a winning habit. We cannot leave our planning in the hands of someone else. Planning creates opportunities which we then must take advantage of. The number of people that do not plan for the future is dramatically high, therefore we must avoid such crowds and associate ourselves with planners, visionaries and more importantly doers, as these are the people that come across a pile of raw material and can visualize a finished product.

Planners make sacrifices and are willing to do the hard things for the promise of enjoying the good life. Planners see a fertile field where others see only futile land. Planners are confident, creative, and disciplined enough to create opportunities that may not be obvious to the masses. A strategic team of a well-established company will create future opportunities through creative marketing; a planner will take into account all the ups and downs of creating a successful ad and will develop strategies that explore outside markets. Planning teaches us to do our homework and to be resourceful in figuring things out before an action is taken. We must plan in preparation for the prosperous future.

Planning also allows for focus of mind and effort. Think of a horse race, for example, in which all the horses wear blinders. The blinders are put on because the goal for the horses is to focus on the finish line. If their vision is not narrowed, they may become distracted and focus elsewhere, which risks losing the race. Although there can be only one winner in a horserace, all the horses, their riders and teams learn something from the experience of being in the race. A horse without blinders, however may drift and not complete the "project" at all.

Build a list and identify the people that you know are planners. Observe the discipline they practice each day to help assure their success. These are the people who plan on a daily, weekly, monthly, and yearly basis so that they remain accountable to their goals and to themselves. These are the people who always have a winning agenda, and no matter how tedious the tasks, they plan and reevaluate the plan until all the pieces of the puzzle come together. The word can't does not exist in the vocabulary of a planner; as he/she will exhaust all resources to figure out ways to work through or around the problem. Planners are by their nature, very optimistic people who create opportunities for themselves and others.

Planners are active individuals who do not wait for an alarm clock to wake them from a deep sleep. They find energy each day to ensure that planning never stops. They carry the past like a text-book and learn from it. They find courage from their past failures, and this resilient winning attitude shows in their success.

Mr. Zeller, a marketing specialist, talks about the importance of having a plan. He explains that to build a house you must first have a foundation, and before building the walls, you must first plan out where the doors and the windows will be installed. Without this plan you might have to take down the walls and start all over again. Mr. Zeller emphasizes being resourceful. Without which, he says, we may jump from task to task without ever completing anything, which is a sure way of missing out on lucrative opportunities. He explains that the need to strategize, compete, to have a clear objective, and to stay active is the key to having a good plan, a solid plan.

If we cannot commit to making the day-to-day plans than we must take a step back and look at the big picture. Choose your own plan, and then make a commitment to stick to it. Never in human history has there been such a time so filled with opportunity and potential. We must free our minds from the past and look to plant seeds that we will harvest in the future. We must look to do the right thing for ourselves, our children, and for our society. The future that comes to fruition is a future we create for ourselves. Being future-consciousness combined with being active and dedicated, will allow us to draw out any picture we want, in any shape we want.

While it might be easy to make plans, it is also easy to fall into the trap of taking on too much. Therefore, be careful in making sure that your plans are realistic and not exaggerated. When creating a plan make sure that you assess your happiness and joy that you want to choose for yourself. If you feel that a certain plan fits your natural aptitude then you can invest energy and time in executing such a plan. A best plan is a plan in which you focus on the concrete steps of the present. Learn from the past and consider the casual variables of the past as they may present in future.

Successful people have a strong will. All others merely have wishes. The best way to construct a plan is to focus on the detailed steps and the contingencies. Avoid any wishful thinking. It is easier for the mind to focus on the concreteness of the plan; a vague plan often leads to confusion and a lack of productivity. A concrete plan takes away the thinking process and automatizes what we want to achieve. It helps avoid any future distractions or temptations which otherwise may divert our attention. Knowing that the goal lies well ahead teaches us self-control.

Psychologists tested the power of instant gratification compared to the long-term vision. In a study, they took a group of children, who ranged in age from four to ten and left in a room with a cookie. The children were told that when the instructor returned in ten minutes, if the child had not eaten the cookie then he or she would receive an additional cookie. Surprisingly, most of the children resisted the temptation and sacrificed immediate gratification for the greater reward. If children can plan for a successful future, so can adults!

Here are three simple steps for planning for a successful future:

1. **The quiet mind**: Spend a few minutes in a quiet environment. Collect and reevaluate your thoughts. Question yourself, think about the bigger picture, find your inner fire, and then get back into the game.

2. **Write it, post it**: If you are a visual learner then write down your thoughts, and post them somewhere you can see every day. Let them be a constant reminder of your goals. Let them be the marching band that plays inside your head!

3. **Navigate**: Navigate your thoughts and plan the route you wish to take on your journey. Slow or fast, it does not matter. What matters is that you try, and also that you try your very best so that there are no regrets in the end.

We have to choose wisely between mere existence and a life of substance. Think about what you can do if you took the liberty to visualize the future and plan for the future. What could you become? What impact could you have on your job and your worth in the marketplace? How could you be different from the rest of the herd? What sort of experience would you have socially? Think of the value you can add to your family. These are the motivating thoughts that drive the winners. Once we understand the power of planning, it is a whole new experience. Planning creates opportunities, which makes us feel good about ourselves and develops a sense of self-worth. In the words of Antoine de Saint-Exupery, "*A goal without a plan is just a wish.*"

Once you can see your future and have plotted its course, it is necessary and pleasurable to keep your hand on the tiller and **keep your perspective aligned**...

24

Keep Your Perspective Aligned

One cool judgment is worth a thousand hasty counsels. | Woodrow T. Wilson

In today's world we are faced with many distractions. High speed internet, a multitude of TV channels, smartphones, FaceBook, Twitter and other social media services all consume much of our time. Add to this the extra tasks we are asked to perform at our jobs, the bills we must pay, family demands, even the extra weight we want to lose or the state of physical fitness we desire. With so much to do it is often easy to get sidetracked and lose prospective of the bigger goals and dreams in life. When you lose perspective, you soon lose sight of the goal altogether. One of the characteristics of perspective is that as you increase the distance from an object, the object becomes smaller and can even disappear from view. When you lose perspective of your dreams and goals, you effectively distance yourself from your desired destination.

The dictionary defines *perspective* as, "A particular attitude towards something, or the way of regarding something." A synonym for perspective is *point of view*. Perspective in the field of art is a representation of an image seen by the eye. In art, for example, perspective is categorized in one-, two-, three-, and four-points.

The one-point perspective is defined as tunnel vision. Imagine standing in a tunnel, where the only thing you can see is the other end. Tunnel vision limits our options and suffocates our chances to grow.

A two-point perspective is like driving down the road and coming to fork in the road. In life we often want more than just two choices. Having to pick either A or B is not sufficient enough and sometimes we must ask for more. After all, if it is something that will determine our success then it is essential to seek a better selection.

Looking up at a tall building describes the three-point perspective. While this view can deliver a great deal of information, the four-point perspective is better yet.

The four-point perspective becomes a panorama that can deliver a 360-degree view. Think about seeing a decision both horizontally and vertically. Think about seeing it from a worm's eye **and** a bird's eye view. The idea here is that we must develop our perspectives by evaluating, assessing, and staying focused.

Behavior is best learned through observation. When we watch the evening news and announcer coverage leads with the headline *Hell on the waters* we begin to imagine all sorts of tragedy. But when the news story unfolds, the reporter describes a cruise to the Bahamas that lost power for two hours before a rescue team saved the day. Was that a stressful two hours for the passengers? Possibly. Blown out of proportion? Absolutely. We must recognize this sort of hyperbole-laden language is being delivered by the media every second of the day, but as a personal responsibility it is our duty to keep our identity intact and to keep things in perspective so that we act accordingly.

We can often recall books, poems and quotes and many other sources of literature that resonate with the very thought we have in mind. We find profound meanings in these writings and often find that they give voice to our thoughts. They help our ideas mature, develop, and blossom. Therefore, we must encourage the habit of reading. We must educate our perspective. Along with action, reading helps us mature our thoughts, build our convictions, and help us develop a 360-degree panoramic view.

Perspective is developed when we ask those questions which start with: Who, What, When, Where, How, and Why. We must not hesitate; we have to be willing to sacrifice our fear of being embarrassed for the good of learning, maturing, and developing. I know of a man who collects quotes. It is his way of honoring the wisdom of the past for the betterment of the future. When asked about perspective he says, "There is no reality, only perception; the world is not necessarily as one perceives it." He further explains that life is a journey and not a destination, and that if we ever felt stuck, we must understand that the barrier only exists in our minds. If we can keep our perspective aligned, we can achieve our goals and our dreams. In order to solidify our perspective, we must study the right books; associate with the right people, and most importantly we must stay focused.

The real fun in the game of life comes from the curve balls that are thrown at us every now and then. While we acknowledge the good times, we must also be prepared for the bad. When things are beyond our control, it is easy to feel defeated, cheated, and helpless. While it is natural to feel this way, we should not overwhelm ourselves with such thoughts. Once we have fully felt the effect of the hardship, we must regain perspective so to make a clear conscious decision.

Although some of our disappointments may not feel temporary, they usually are. We all experience problems from time to time. But the way in which we handle our problems can vary greatly. Take the example of two brothers, each of whom gets a speeding ticket on the way to work. The elder brother's entire day is ruined. He whines and complains about his despicable luck for hours, spreading a negative vibe wherever he can and accomplishes very little at work. The other brother, however, treats the speeding ticket as a deserving nuisance. He acknowledges his mistake, makes a promise to himself that he will not repeat such behavior again and quickly moves on.

As we broaden the scope of our perception, we experience less stress, an improved attitude, and more joy in daily activities. There are wonderful things around us. All we have to do is to allow ourselves time to perceive them. Let go of the negative, and embrace the positive. Those people with a positive outlook on life will remind you that things happen for a reason. The key is not to become more rigid in your approach to life, but to be more flexible, open-minded, tolerant, and to cultivate your spirituality along the way.

The higher power serves a reminder that we are being looked after. It is a refreshing and an unbelievably strong motivation. This spiritual belief offers the weak the chance to be strong, the shallow the opportunity to be bold, and the wicked to be good. Spirituality helps nurture our perspective. It lets good prevail.

Perspective is a fluid concept. It is an ongoing battle with the self. It is a key factor in deciding our fate. Therefore, let us strive for the bigger picture; let our maturity develop our outlook so that we may keep our perspectives aligned. In the words of Steve Jobs, *"A lot of people in our industry haven't had very diverse experiences. So they don't have enough dots to connect, and they end up with very linear solutions without a broad perspective on the problem. The broader that one's understanding of the human experience is, the better design we will have."*

Luck favors the well-prepared. There is always opportunity to seize upon new developments **and seize the moment**...

25

Seize the Moment

Seize the day and put the least possible trust in tomorrow | Horace

No opportunity is lost; it's only that the other fellow takes it. From the standpoint of an opportunity, much has been said about seizing the moment and achieving happiness. Like a lion quietly stalking its prey before it seizes the opportunity to attack, successful people of the past and the present are driven by an internal impulse to seize as much as they can, whenever they can. It is an impulse that sleeps with one eye open.

Successful people enjoy their jobs, families, good health, friends, social gatherings and all other aspects of their lives, because of one simple gift. This is the gift of taking the ordinary and making it extraordinary. We all have this gift, but the only thing that separates the average person from the successful one is the law of action. It is when we act, we conquer. Successful people make and create opportunities, while the average person merely waits for opportunities to come to them. Instead of wishing for fewer problems, we should wish for more skills so that each minute is more productive than the next. Instead of asking God for more time, we should ask ourselves for more work in an hour. Let us not allow our wishful thinking to seize our lives, let us reverse this process and seize our wishful thinking by turning it into reality.

A person who does not feel particularly blessed might ask, "I am not successful so how do I turn ordinary to extraordinary?" As previously mentioned, it is done through the law of action. Opportunity constantly presents itself—in weakness, in sickness, in need, in giving, and in receiving. We can seize the moment simply by returning a smile, offering a helping hand, tending to the sick, paying respect to the elderly and by paying attention to our loved ones or those around us.

We must see every act as an opportunity so that we can learn to seize the *now*, in order that we can grow mentally, emotionally, and spiritually. With each charitable act we can learn to seize the joy of kindness. With each smile we can learn to seize happiness. By paying respect we can learn to seize the gift of dignity. These are the tools needed to build a strong foundation, and once this foundation is built, the materialistic gains follow.

Each day presents its own gifts and we must learn to make the most of them. We cannot give into complaining, because often the mistakes we regret are the ones we did not commit. Other actions are not mistakes at all; they are simply actions that are unusual for us. So be bold and commit the so-called *mistake* of leaving your comfort zone to do the hard thing. Be bold and commit the *mistake* of working more than you are being paid for. Be bold and commit the *mistake* of studying when you could easily watch TV. Be courageous and commit the *mistake* of being moral, when everyone else thinks the handicapped parking sign does not apply to them. Give to charity. Prepare to seize every opportunity and hasten your search to find and adapt the right personal philosophy.

If you are not willing to risk the unusual, you will have to settle for the ordinary. Life is short and you cannot spend it just thinking or trying to avert every possible risk. You must act, which sometimes includes taking risks. By the way, planning as I have already mentioned, is an essential part of doing. Let us skip the daily routine of frowning, let us move past the feeling of envy, and let us pave the way for our positive entity to take over, because it is the only way to seize the good we seek. Here is what Napoleon Hill writes about the phrase, Do it now! "*It can affect every phase of your life. It* can help you do the things you should do but don't feel like doing. It can keep you from procrastinating when an unpleasant duty faces you. But it can also help you do those things that you want to do. It helps you seize those precious moments that, if lost, may never be retrieved."

A touching reminder of the importance of seizing the moment comes from the mother of a twenty-three year old who was killed during a robbery. The mother's agony over her son's death and her plea for his return was painful to witness. Life is short. We must seize each day. We must love; we must live and pay heed to those we care for. This young man was only twenty-three years old. He had barely begun life as an adult, as his mother often recalls. He was still only opening his eyes and waking up to adulthood. The mother's pain and the rest of the family's grief is a reminder that life is a wisp of air that cannot be retrieved once it passes us by.

Life can be pushed by drive as much as it can be pulled by goals. In the words of Maxwell Maltz, "What is opportunity, and when does it knock? It never knocks. You can wait a whole lifetime, listening, hoping, and you will hear no knocking. None whatsoever. You are opportunity, and you must knock on the door leading to your destiny. You prepare yourself to recognize opportunity, to pursue and seize opportunity as you develop the strength of your personality, and build a self-image with which you are able to live; with your self-respect alive and growing."

While we may arrive late to the game of life, rest assured it will proceed as scheduled. In the words of Wayne Dyer, "You'll seldom experience regret for anything that you've done. It is what you haven't done that will torment you. The message, therefore, is clear. Do it! Develop an appreciation for the present moment. Seize every second of your life and savor it. Value your present moments. Wasting them through self-defeating ways means you've lost them forever."

As these talents and skills grow within you, so it becomes easier to visualize and **see clearly**...

26

Clarity

Wisdom and compassion flow from simplicity and clarity; from having nothing to prove and nothing to defend. | Barry Magid

"Why does he have more than I do? Why am I not as lucky?" At one time or another such thoughts may cross our mind. We may become resentful because of a perceived lack in our own lives. We may self-scrutinize for not being good enough, or rich enough, or healthy enough. Despite the fact that we all think we are good and moral, luck may think otherwise.

A simple explanation of this perceived injustice lies in they way we define *musts* and *shoulds*. To live an extraordinary life we must have an extraordinary philosophy, and to have an extraordinary philosophy we need to be alert and at the same time educate the state of our minds, the state of our health, and the state of our environment. Even though we possess the ability and the strength to attain these lofty states, surprisingly not everyone has a desire to attain such standards. Society will pay the price we hold ourselves to. If we sell ourselves short, further discount requests will be made. If we sell ourselves on par with the value of a diamond, then all would pay as if their money could not be spent on anything more valuable.

The secret of personal value lies in having clear goals in life. A person cannot be a good father without caring to know what it is that his children want. A jockey will tell you about the ways to prepare the horse for a race. From grooming the horse to feeding, mucking, handling and caring for its feet by packing them with mud, a jockey understands that while all horses run, the victory comes in paying attention to the details.

Our brains work more efficiently if we clarify our goals by paying attention to the details. Clear goals and objectives are essential to success. If we do not clarify what goals we are trying to accomplish, then we'll spend our lives unwittingly helping others achieve theirs. The difference between having a direction and having a goal is clarity. *Direction* means walking East or West. *Goal* on the other hand has only one meaning; being on top of the Statue of Liberty.

The way to go from where you are, to where you want to be, is by knowing what you want. Clarity is power. Don't wake up tomorrow as if it is just another day, just to see what life might bring. Rise to a new day with a purpose. How much longer will you walk up the flight of stairs only to find out that it was the wrong staircase? Being clear with your goals requires active participation in your own life. It requires making a choice rather than waiting for a surprise or a gift. Like a pilot adjusting the heading of a plane as it flies through wind and weather, having a clear goal serves as a navigator. It helps you adjust your heading over and over again, in order to stay on course. Whether the goal is to lose weight, evaluate self-discipline, or get more done in a day, it is best to calculate progress on a numerical scale of one to ten, and adjust the headings as needed. In the words of Conan O'Brien, "The beauty is that through disappointment you can gain clarity, and with clarity comes conviction and true originality."

I'll worry when I have time.

To start the process of building for the future, we create imaginary roadmaps and bridges that tie together all of our scattered ideas and resources. However, during the building process, we frequently fear the future – the unknown. We become anxious about the *but*'s and the *what if*'s. We say to ourselves, "But I am not sure if I can get the job done," or "What if I can't get that job?" These are the worries and concerns for the future, and, in certain situations, such concerns can be necessary and helpful. But when these emotions run loose and take hold of our lives, then that becomes worry in itself. If we worry more about failing than accomplishing the task in front of us, then failure gets the upper hand. Much of what we worry about has to do with losing what we have. We are afraid to lose, whether it is our power, wealth, health, freedom, family or even life itself. But the knowledge that we are mortal presents us the opportunity to live life fully, to choose action over inaction, and work over procrastination. Therefore, awareness of mortality is a blessing and not a curse.

Many people start their day by worrying, but this will not make things better, it will only make things worse. The stress of traffic consumes people in the morning, as does the pressure of work throughout the day, which leads to inadequate sleep at night. Many of us even recognize our unhealthy worrying patterns and long for it to go away.

Worry is exhausting but action is liberating and energizing. If you worry constantly about losing a job, it sets the stage for losing it. However, if the same energy is channeled into learning a skill or fixing a problem at work, it turns the liability of worry into an asset of ability.

Life teaches us that everything worth having is worth striving for. No other pursuit is more worthy of our efforts than investing our time and energy into creating a life of extraordinary quality and value. However, such ambition and drive requires a strong will and sound state of mind: a mind that is full of thoughts and free of worries. The inability to tolerate uncertainty impacts anxiety and worry. It does not matter what the outcome of an anticipated project, interview or an event is; what matters is whether or not we did the best we could.

Our worries and anxieties are a lot like plants; they grow if we water them, care for them, and nurture them.. In order to gain peace of mind, we need to stop acting like a god trying to fix the problems of the universe. We need simply to keep ourselves busy with worthy actions.

In 1973, Dr. Grossarth-Maticek performed a study on twelve hundred people to test the factors affecting the longevity of their lives. These people were given tests that asked questions about goals, social connections, the ability to express themselves, relationships, reactions to situations, and overall feelings of self. After dividing the participants into two even groups, he provided one group with a self-help brochure and six one-hour training sessions over a period of a year. The other group was either given placebo training or no training at all. When Dr. Grossarth-Maticek checked in on the health of the participants some thirteen years later, he found that the four-hundred and nine people who given the training were still alive and healthy versus only ninety-seven people in the group that had received no training. Based on this and other similar research, Thomas R. Blakeslee, author of *The Attitude Factor: Extend Your Life by Changing the Way You Think*, believes that attitude can create a powerful emotional response that strongly affects the immune system, circulatory system, and even the risk of accidents.

We need to be mindful of how we handle stress. Overgeneralizing, as in, "I'll never get that job," personalization, as in, "I am responsible for my relative's death," labeling, as in, "I am worthless; a failure; clumsy," and jumping to conclusions, as in, "I can tell he hates me," are feelings that diminish positivity and in turn create doubt. Letting go of anxious thoughts is a helpful technique for dealing with stressful moments. By keeping your mind and body in the present moment you can realign drifting focus and help generate solutions to real problems.

Many people believe that worrying is essential in order to stay ahead in the game; they believe that when used constructively, worrying can produce the winning edge. This idea is only half correct: the winning edge does not go to the one who worries, it goes to their competition. No boxer goes into the ring thinking that worrying gives him the winning edge.

While life presents problems and worries, it also presents us with the tools to deal with these scenarios. This starts by asking the right questions. "Where should I look first to find these tools? How can I become better?" A worried mind occupied by the thought of loss prevents the pleasure of gain. As Ralph Waldo Emerson writes, "Some of your hurts you have cured, and the sharpest you still have survived, but what torments of grief you endured from the evil which never arrived." In the words of Thomas Jefferson, "How much pain they have cost us, the evils which have never happened."

Of the many virtues that fill up a completed person, one of the most valuable is **kindness**...

27

Kindness

*Kindness is the language that the deaf can hear and the blind can see |
Mark Twain*

Kindness is the universal language that can be seen, heard, and felt.
While much of this focuses on personal achievements, success requires
that we build working relationship with others, and there is no better
way to build working relationships than with a genuine act of kindness.

Real kindness represents the sort of benevolence and selflessness
that increases our faith in humanity. It is genuine care without
personal motives. It is the act displayed when no one is looking.
Kindness can take on many different disguises. A genuine act of
kindness can serve as an intelligent sympathy to those in distress. It
can assign worthy motives. It can start charities and build empires.
It springs love, care, compassion and tolerance. Kindness is about
caring for others far beyond what we think they might deserve.
Much like the intensity of the sun, kindness is very intense. Ice left
long enough in the sun will melt. Similarly kindness can turn hate
into love, intolerance into acceptance, and anger into forgiveness.

Each of us owes it to everyone else to be as kind as possible, as
often as possible. This is a healthy habit and it produces real results.
A kind word goes a long way. It can make another person's day
worthwhile and leave a lasting impression.

Gary, a friend of mine, took a recent trip to New York City where he met an older cab driver who picked him up from the airport and took him to midtown Manhattan. During the ride, Gary shared a few words with the cab driver and found out that he was suffering from cancer. The driver was working to maintain his family back in The Republic of Congo. Instead of enjoying the sights of New York City, Gary listened carefully to the cab driver's touching story and offered advice and genuine praise for his perseverance. After reaching his destination, Gary offered a handsome tip. The cab driver politely refused the tip and instead waived the fare. This interaction reminds us that a kind act goes a long way.

Kindness is never wasted; it is always invested. Kindness is an act that has equal importance to living as does breathing. It is important to every aspect of life. If it is performed long enough, kindness can become ingrained. Seeking the best in others and covering up their faults helps to cultivate kindness. The more good we seek out in others, the more that good will translate into our lives and onto our daily activities.

The warm feeling of kindness frees us from the shackles of resentment, jealousy, suspicion, and manipulation. Instead it cultivates loyalty, respect, patience and appreciation. We should always offer kindness to ourselves, as well. Being kind to yourself allows you to see what causes pain and conflict, and it further empowers you to embrace any contradictions and inconsistencies.

Kindness can elevate self-knowledge to allow room for improvement. Giving kindness to yourself is to embrace yourself, to reach out to other people with great strength and awareness.

How often do you find yourself in situations where you are desperate to rush off even though the other person might be feeling as if their life has come apart? How much do you care to listen to those in need? How often do you find yourself wandering off into your own thoughts and worries while someone else is sharing their troubles with you? The charitable gift of kindness can only be given when you present yourself fully in the moment. Listening to others and caring for their concern is the best gift any human can offer to another. Just think of the impact the kindest people have on your life. The joy and the happiness they bring is very fulfilling. You too can have similar impact on others when you decide to act out of kindness. Kindness is a supreme state of health and a prosperous state of mind. One kind act is a self-esteem booster. It is true that everyone fights fear, hurt, pain, and disappointments on a daily basis. But this allows us to be someone's hero everyday through the simple act of kindness. Contrary to the popular belief, a hero does not wear a cape or possess any super powers. A hero dresses just like you and me and carries a smile on his/her face and compassion in the heart. We all have the ability to do great things, and all it takes is one act of kindness.

In the words of the Dalai Lama, "Whether one believes in a religion or not, and whether one believes in rebirth or not, there isn't anyone who doesn't appreciate kindness and compassion." The great sales guru and speaker Og Mandino writes, "*Beginning today, treat everyone you meet as if they were going to be dead by midnight. Extend to them all the care, kindness and understanding you can muster, and do it with no thought of any reward. Your life will never be the same again.*"

Just like kindness, the capacity to think, feel and **wait**, builds bridges across to others…

28

Patience

A man who is a master of patience is master of everything else. | *George Savile*

The old cliché *patience is a virtue* might be a tough pill to swallow. The reason is quite simple. We live in an era where advertisements and newsfeeds condition us for immediate gratification. We no longer need cash to make a purchase – we have credit cards. Instead of controlling and educating our urges, we give in easily in order to avoid disappointment or frustration.

This approach might satisfy us for the present moment, but it has the effect of turning each of us into a slave to our urges. Patience is indeed a virtue but it is not a fundamental virtue. Other qualities like self-control, humility, and generosity are the building blocks. If the scriptures serve any witness then Buddha, Jesus, Moses, and Mohammad (PBUH) personified these qualities. Despite the laziness, selfishness, and the ignorance of their disciples, these figures refused to complain or resent their followers. Instead they showed self-control and taught the word of God to those who did not believe. Their willingness to lower themselves to the level of the people shows the humility of their strong character. The scriptures bear witness to their generous approach for the poor, sick, and the needy. The patience practiced by these role models is timeless and exceptional. Therefore, in order to perfect the art of patience, we must practice generosity, humility and finally self-control.

In order to practice patience we must first come to realize the things that irritate us the most. Whether it is the presence of another person, a certain feeling or a particular circumstance, complaining about the fiddling little details or backbiting is a petty form of grievance guaranteed to backfire.

For example: A young student approached his professor to ask for an extra credit activity since he had failed his exam. The professor was reluctant but said that he would consider the request and would answer the following week. The student made up his mind and thought for sure that the professor had meant to say 'no'. In the following days the student spread unpleasant rumors about the professor, and soon enough the entire class had heard them. The professor also heard of the unpleasant rumors but he stayed calm and poised. Instead he told the student to proceed with the extra credit project so as to improve his overall grade. The student, feeling guilty on the inside, left only to return after a few days to apologize for the rumors he had spread. To this the teacher asked the student to take a handful of small feathers and release them out the window. After releasing all the tiny feathers, the student returned and said, "I have done what you asked me to do." The professor now told the student to go and collect all the feathers and bring them back. The student said, "That is not possible. The wind has blown all of them away." In response the professor said, "Well now you are learning. Once words leave the tongue they cannot be retrieved; they spread all over just like feathers on the wind." Had the student been patient and showed self-control even during his state of uncertainty, he could have spared himself humiliation and embarrassment.

Complaining creates an unfriendly and an unpleasant environment that offers little room for success. This is not to say we should not complain about unjust events, but we should use sound judgment between right and wrong as the basis of the complaint. Otherwise, it is better to remain patient and wait out the storm. People often become impatient with the teenager in the house, the traffic on the street, the coworker delaying the project, or the long line at the bank, supermarket or tollbooth. Losing patience is to lose peace of mind. It is not adversity that robs us of all our virtues, but the impatient behavior.

We are all driven by personal motives and desires. And when something gets in the way of our plans or our plans do not go the way we had hoped, we become uncertain. A state of panic takes over. It is important that we remind ourselves during these moments to stay calm and poised, to re-strategize and to reconsider the chosen path. While standing in lines or stuck in traffic, we must all come to a realization that all the other people waiting are equally worthy and deserving. Not everyone possesses our strengths or our weaknesses. Our kids, spouse, friends, family, colleagues, and neighbors, all learn at their own pace. Give them the time, the knowledge, and the required resources to grow. Be patient.

Everything we do, say, or hear counts. It is important to avoid speaking or making important decisions when you are under stressful or intense emotions. Decisions made under such circumstances can leave us with remorse and shame. It is better to let the storm pass and allow for peace to return. What we say and do always defines who we are.

Day by day, week-by-week, month-by-month, persistence and patience help us to shape the ideal character. We cannot grow as prosperous human beings without patience. Life's lessons do not always present themselves clearly. We must wait patiently and then act quickly once the door of opportunity presents itself.

Along with being patient is the importance of being aware. Be aware and listen to everything going on around you. Observe, and look for the opportunities in disguise. If you are patient and keep your thoughts to yourself while the other person is talking, you might learn something new, or spy something valuable.

Here are three helpful tips to becoming more patient:

1. Stop & Go: Create some space between your initial impulse and your action. Take slow deep breaths and count to 10. This helps slow your heart rate, relaxes your body, and gives you some emotional distance from the situation. Once you have control of your emotions you can get back to issue at hand.

2. Talk to yourself. Listen to your best friend: yourself. Tell yourself that whatever it is, it can wait until you make up your mind on what to do about it. Evaluate the activity and then reconsider your action. If it is someone you are angry with, ask yourself whether yelling and screaming at this person is worth it. Will it still be worth the trouble a year from now?

3. Listen then speak: While what you have to say may be extremely valuable, remember that the person you are speaking to is also a human being who might share the same sentiment. Or they might not. Do not forget the common courtesy of listening. This practice allows you to develop patience and strengthens your relationship with the listener. Patiently plan your response to what the other person is saying; there is no need for a rushed response. One thoughtful response is better than a thousand thoughtless ideas combined.

In the words of L.G. Lovasik, "The practice of patience toward one another, the overlooking of one another's defects, and the bearing of one another's burdens is the most elementary condition of all human and social activity in the family, in the professions, and in society."

Sometimes, all does not go well but vision and planning go far to lessen the **damage**....

29

Adversity

Prosperity is a great teacher, but adversity is greater. Possession pampers the mind; privation trains and strengthens it. | William Hazlitt

We are all students of life, and we make decisions to learn or not learn from our experiences. The standards to which we want to uphold our lives depend on the choices we make when faced with trials and difficulties.

Like love and happiness, adversity is also part of life. Rejecting this fact is foolish and dangerous. In its present form hardship may feel like an undeserving misfortune without any useful scientific value. But in reality, adversity tests the essence of a person.

When the rubber meets the road, when the cards have been dealt, when the time to touch gloves and fight is upon us, it is then that adversity will challenge the core of our character. Adversity is a mirror that reflects the outside image and transfers it over to the inside. It shakes us upside-down like a ketchup bottle. It sometimes seems like for every ten steps forward, we are sent nine steps back. Adversity and difficulties test patience, endurance, and faith. Often we are still dealing with one problem when another hurdle comes along, leaving us feeling worn out and exhausted.

These painful events lead us to ask a very familiar, yet very important question, "Why me?" Perhaps the answer to this question lies in knowing who benefits from adversity. (Hint: It's you.) We all face adversity. The need for adversity is as important as the body's need for food, and the soul's need for peace. Learning to deal with its different consequences makes us who we are. Every difficult situation we confront in life strengthens the will and the confidence to rise to any challenge, no matter the size or its invisible strength. Scrutinizing life for being unfair or unjust serves no purpose. In fact when we consume ourselves with such petty thoughts, we run the risk of overlooking the opportunity for wisdom and growth, which come disguised as problems. When adversity approaches, we should not shrink away, but instead extend our internal faith – the faith that shouts, *"I am bigger and stronger than any problem"* – to every cell in the body. Adversity is like a rain that washes off the dust so that we may see how valuable we really are.

Jaime was a young boy from Missouri who lost his legs in a fire. After being bedridden for nearly three years, he found the strength to walk again and took up sports only to become the fastest runner in the entire township. His spirit to not quit even though many thought he would never walk again, is a reminder that we are all as free as our well-developed alternatives. If we limit our options than we certainly limit our progress and our growth. Developing more skills and increasing our options can help us cope with stressful moments and make the best use of time and opportunity. Everyone faces problems—from the most successful to the least. However, the defining act between the two is that successful people respond more resourcefully, more quickly and in a more positive way.

Adversity gives way to understanding, tolerance, and acceptance. It has a mysterious way of unfolding a person's greatness. Like martial arts teaches lessons for remaining calm and poised during adversity, life teaches a similar lesson to those who are willing to learn. Like moving up the ranks in karate through discipline and hard work, life also requires us to be disciplined and persistent in pursuit of the good life. Henry Fielding writes, *"He that can heroically endure adversity will bear prosperity with equal greatness of soul; for the mind that cannot be dejected by the former is not likely to be transported by the latter."*

The birth of the "Oklahoma Standard" after the 1995 Oklahoma City bombing symbolizes the growth of a nation to come together in the face of adversity, to lift the spirits of those in need. It symbolizes resilience and teaches us the important lesson of dealing with setbacks without feeling defeated. It teaches us to be considerate, compassionate, and most importantly to be strong. Rose Kennedy writes, "Prosperity tries the fortunate, adversity the great." Robert Collier adds, *"In every adversity there lies the seed of an equivalent advantage. In every defeat is a lesson showing you how to win the victory next time."*

All of these ideas need a **structure**, a story of your life yet to be lived...

30

The Right Personal Plan

If you don't design your own life plan, chances are you'll fall into someone else's plan. And guess what they have planned for you? Not much. | *Jim Rohn*

A whale is as unique as a cactus, but expecting a whale to survive in the desert would be a major error in judgment. Similarly we all have talents—where and how we use them determines what we will get out of them.

Our everyday life is influenced by the decisions we make, the people we associate with, and the things we do. Our choices, ideas, attitude, and beliefs determine the life we live. Rather than thinking and then acting, we too often simply react. To react is not necessarily a bad thing, but whether that reaction causes benefit or harm depends on our personal philosophy. Developing the right personal philosophy is like developing a habit, and doing something out of habit is second nature, and therefore, easy. The idea of developing the right personal philosophy is like having the right personal plan. Having the right personal plan is essential for making good personal choices. With the right plan we can guide our instincts, our reactions, our impulses, and most importantly our decisions.

To live an inspired life we must first observe our everyday lives. From the very first thought that enters our mind when we wake up, to the very last thought of the day before we go to sleep, our lives play out exactly as we plan them. The fine line between success and failure lies in the thoughts that guide us. Like the right diet for a short distance runner, and the powerful engines that lift an airplane high above the ground, the right personal plan is an essential fuel for developing a healthy state of mind. This will facilitate the ambition for success and allows us to soar above and beyond our wildest imaginations. By making the right choices, we can live our dream every day.

We all have some sort of philosophy, whether it's cultural or personal. One way or another we all hold different belief and thoughts. What is important is to determine whether or not our personal plan serves us, or do we serve it? While the former is desirable, the latter leads down to a lonely, dark alley. A good personal plan assures good actions which leads to good results. By assessing your contentment with a job or lifestyle is the measurement against which one can determine the need for change. Our society's demand for rapid growth requires that we develop new skills and abilities in order to retain the slight edge in life. The fact that Mother Earth does not have enough resources to give in abundance is a pretense used by those with poor or no personal plan to hide their own failure. These are the people that have not changed or further developed their personal plans to make the best use of what life has to offer. In a rapidly moving society, these people seem to be standing still due to their outdated, obstructive, self-destructive, or in plain words "bad" personal philosophies. Success is obtainable if we commit ourselves to the philosophy of change and action. We achieve abundance through commitment and solidarity.

As part of a documentary, a film director gave a homeless man $100,000 in order to test how the homeless man would spend the money. The homeless man did not know that he was going to receive the money. He was only told that he would be filmed as part of a documentary that showed how a homeless man spends his days. It was about the day and life of a homeless person. The homeless man "found" a briefcase with money in a garbage bin while looking for soda cans to sell. He was clearly broke and when he found the briefcase with the money in it, he could not believe it. In shock because of his good fortune, he broke down into tears. What the homeless man did next with his money was no surprise considering he had a poor personal philosophy.

The homeless man bought himself a car, rented an apartment, bought his friends brand new cars, and bought more and more things until he had spent all the money. Despite the film director's offer to provide a financial advisor and counselor for free, the homeless man continued to spend until he was left with nothing. Within only a few months, he had lost everything and stated that he was back on the streets and homeless again. This was a painful reminder of what a lack of good personal plan can lead to. Often rich athletes declare bankruptcy or other sorts of financial setbacks not because they don't have enough but because of a lack of a good personal philosophy.

Here is a list of questions we must ask ourselves in order to understand our personal philosophy:

- What do we envision ourselves doing while getting up each and every morning? Is there some motive? If so what is the motive?

- What drives our motives? Is it family? Friends? Personal beliefs? Deep down, what is it that makes us want to do the thing we feel most obligated to?

- How satisfied do we feel at the end of each day?

- What makes our beliefs so important to us? What is it about our beliefs that make them the core principle of our lives? How much good do our beliefs serve, either for others or us?

- Do our beliefs measure up to the higher standards required to live a fulfilled life? Is prosperity attainable with our beliefs? Could we live a fulfilled life with our current thought process?

Once we choose a personal plan that empowers rather than limit us, we can begin to act in line with our new beliefs. Choosing the right personal plan is a process that takes time, patience, self-awareness and perseverance. Developing a vision, and then changing one thought at a time creates the right personal plan.

Procrastination, lack of self-reliance, and laboring dreadfully are poisons that we cannot afford to drink if prosperity is the ultimate goal. These are the evils that hold out all opportunities and only bring in disappointment.

Having the right personal philosophy can teach us how to be breathtakingly great in all that we do. It teaches us to make small changes one at a time. We must create and educate our personal philosophy in preparation for a better future.

The importance of developing a personal philosophy is the determining factor between failure and success. Coach Pete Carroll had tremendous success at the University of Southern California as a football coach, even though he was an average NFL coach. After getting fired by the New England Patriots in 1999, coach Carroll did some soul searching and developed his *"Doing things better than they've ever been done before"* and *"Always compete"* personal philosophy. Soon he found himself as the head coach of the University of Southern California college football team that won back-to-back national championships titles. He attributes his success to his personal philosophy, which helped him develop a championship caliber team.

With the right mindset and the right personal plan, we can achieve greatness. We can conquer heaven, and we can live each day in abundance. Eleanor Roosevelt writes, *"One's philosophy is not best expressed in words; it is expressed in the choices one makes... and the choices we make are ultimately our responsibility."*

Now, it's time to put this all together...

31

Now Go!

Failure is simply the opportunity to begin again, this time more intelligently | Henry Ford

There is a remarkable border between success and failure, and it is demarcated by the attitudes that I have described in this book. Think, for example about the difference between a wealthy person and a poor person. A poor person looks for ways to save money, while a wealthy person looks for ways to make money. When a poor-minded person looks at an opportunity that involves risk, he or she will ask, "How much will this cost?" whereas a rich-minded person will ask, "How much could this earn?" Now, of course, a poor person has to watch every penny much more closely, but in this country any poor person can become rich, and any rich person can become poor through actions and attitudes. They are separated by expectation and attitude, by optimism and belief.

A magnet can lift objects ten times its weight. The same can be said of a fulcrum or a lever. And the same can be said of a human being. The seemingly impossible can be achieved when it is approached just right.

With each success, your mind will change. It will develop a confidence that leads to the expectation that you can succeed, and yes, actually, you deserve to succeed! These positive vibrations are then picked up by others; not in any sort of cosmic way, but simply through body language, eye contact, and a tone of voice, choice of words, facial expressions and the overall willingness that your mind and body demonstrates. This expectation does not demonstrate greed or selfishness. It is a positive embrace of the fact that good things can happen when you see beyond obstacles and can actually connect with your own life path.

The good news is it costs nothing to start. It requires simply that you practice the attitudes and approaches that I have described here. Listen to stories about other people's successes and failures. Read biographies. Identify role models that you would like to emulate and equally importantly, identify those whose attributes you would not like to share. Decide which attributes you do not want others to see in you.

There will always be people around who got a better break than you, who were born richer, who were handed privilege and opportunity without deserving or appreciating it. But for all their wealth, many of them are shallow and unhappy. But the people who achieve success on their own terms — and this does not solely refer to money — are people who appreciate their success, because they hold on to the precious raw material that got them there.

Opportunities seem to multiply as they are seized. As Henry Ford once said, "*The harder I work, the luckier I get.*"

You have that chance. And now is as good a time as any to take it and make it work for you. So go! Do good things. Enjoy the rewards. And share your energy with anyone and everyone. It's really amazing what will happen.

[1] The data from WebMd can be found here:
http://www.webmd.com/balance/features/science-good-deeds

[i] Luutonen S (2007) Anger and depression – theoretical and clinical considerations. Nordic Journal of Psychiatry; 61: 246–51.

CPSIA information can be obtained
at www.ICGtesting.com
Printed in the USA
FSOW03n2340140318
45739FS